Stop Overthinking

How to Stop Negative Thinking, Reduce Anxiety and Stress. The Power of Positive Thinking Helps Your Body and Your Brain to Live Happy

Table of Contents

Introduction

When talking about procrastination, everyone might relate to it because there's none who could deny it. At least, once or twice in your life, procrastination would have played its role. Whenever you miss your deadlines, the level of anxiety rises above your head and you are forced to complete the project as soon as possible. But deep down, you know it is impossible to complete because there is so much to do. Yet, you try! Procrastination will make your life miserable, so try not to make it a habit.

Some people want to stop procrastinating, but they are unable to because they don't know how to do it. Or sometimes, they might be missing the motivation they need. And it can be frustrating, I know. You must understand the fact that procrastinating factors differ from individual to another:

A writer will procrastinate on the project he/she was assigned. And then, he/she must work day and night to complete the project.

A student will delay school work and then, complete at the last moment.

An athlete will delay medications because he is so concerned about the current game.

If you evaluate each example above, you will understand that through procrastination every individual mention in the example will be affected. For instance, the athlete will have to deal with a lot of severe issues if he doesn't treat the injury right away. Likewise, there will be a lot of emotional drawbacks as well.

I'll share some of the practical daily practices that you can follow to overcome procrastination. These practices will help you beat procrastination even if you are feeling lazy or unmotivated. Before you begin reading the practices below, you must bear in mind that you can select any of the following practices. This means you are not forced to practice all the habits below. Let's get started!

- Find solutions to potential emergencies

Procrastination is not a simple bad habit; rather it is dangerous. It will have a huge impact on your health. Sometimes, you might even lose the great bonds that you shared with your family members. They might even come to a point where they assume that you no longer care. There will be situations in life where you have to deal with unexpected priorities such as death, sickness, and much more. Such situations can't wait because you will have to address them immediately. In such an instance, you would have to drop all the scheduled tasks. Some other times, great family events might turn into dreadful situations, and you can't avoid them and get back to your work. Emergencies don't come with a warning, so you have to put up with the obstacles it creates. How can you avoid emergencies? Are you going to stop everything and address the issue? Or if you have already delayed the work and then, something urgent comes up, how are you planning to handle it? What might happen when you ignore the emergencies?

To handle emergencies, you have to have a clear picture of the type of emergencies that you are dealing with. You can think about the aftereffects of avoiding the emergency. Or think about the people who are related to the emergency, how will they feel if you ignore it? What are the actions that you can take to solve this emergency issue so that you can get back to work? Or can you put off the emergency issue because it is not life-threatening?

Before you dig in further, let me tell you. If you are working so hard that you don't even have time for your family, it means you are losing a lot of good things in life. You are not actually living your life — this where the concept of smart working comes into the picture. You can easily get busy and forget about the people around you. Or you can easily put off emergencies that you believed as not important, and those emergencies might actually turn out severe. Of course, you might be so busy that you don't even have time for important things, but it is all about your priorities.

No project, appointment, or meeting is worth ignoring for the emergencies that might affect the life of a loved one. I'd suggest stopping other things when something urgent comes up because procrastination is not only about work but also about life. If you address emergencies right away, you wouldn't have to deal with the worst cases down the line.

Most of the time, we think procrastination is all about work and how we delay work. But here I pointed out something that you should consider.

Basically, if you organize work-related activities and complete before the deadline, or if you have completed half the work already, unexpected priorities might not create a huge impact on your work life. What matters is being organized and knowing how to prioritize your life matters.

- 2.   Do daily review

Another best way to avoid procrastination is through daily reviews. If you allocate ten minutes from your day, you can do the review. When you are doing the review, you will be able to find the priorities of your day. Then, you can analyze the tasks that will have a huge impact on your short-term goals. To make this review session simpler, consider carrying out a Q&A format. What are the scheduled meetings that you need to attend? Are there any emails that you must reply to today? Are there any documents that need to be edited today? Are there any appointments that will take more time than you allocated? What are the tasks that require more attention?

Likewise, you must do a Q&A to find out the layout of the day. But you don't have to stick the questions that I have mentioned. Instead, you can prepare your own Q&A and follow it. If you do this daily review, you will be able to understand the layout for the day. When you have a layout, you will be able to stay on the track. You will have proper knowledge of the tasks that need more time or a quick response. Hence, you will not procrastinate because you are aware that it will impact your goals negatively.

If you want to know one of the best concepts that beat procrastination, it will be the Pareto Principle. This is all about 80/20 rule. Try to learn more about this concept before you actually apply it on your day to day activities.

- 3. MIT's or the Most Important Tasks

It's tough to beat procrastination if you begin your day with a to-do-list that burst out with tasks. You must have a simplified to-do-list if you want to get things done on time and correctly. How can you simplify your to-do-list? It is pretty simple if you focus on MIT's - most important tasks. You have to settle for the tasks that will have a considerable impact on your long term goals. This is recommended by many experts who focus on productivity.

My tips are to select the top three important tasks that need to be handled by the end of the day. It is better to pick two important tasks that have tight deadlines and another that will impact your long-term career goal. If you keep an eye on MIT's concept, you will be able to curb procrastination. Once you complete the two most important activities of your day, you will be interested in doing the other activities by the end of the day. And that motivation is very much needed if you want to succeed in beating procrastination.

- 4. The Eisenhower Matrix

Of course, who doesn't like productivity? You'd be glad if things happen the way you planned. But sometimes, things don't work as you planned. If your life is also like mine, filled with constant emergencies and changes, you must have the ability to make quick decisions.

If you want to make a quick decision, you need the support from the Eisenhower Matrix. The founder of this concept was in the army. It was the reason why he invented this concept. It's not possible to work according to the plan when you are in an army. There will be sudden changes and importance. In such an instance, the Eisenhower Matrix concept was the guideline.

If Eisenhower utilized this in the army, why can't you utilize this in your life to avoid procrastination? When you are dealing with this concept, you shouldn't forget the four quadrants related to it. By focusing on the four quadrants, you will be able to approach your day to day tasks accordingly. Let me mention the four quadrants in detail:

Quadrant 1: Urgent plus important

These are the tasks that need to be completed first because they are way important than any other tasks and they directly deal with your career goals. Plus, you must complete the tasks right away because they are urgent. If you complete these tasks, you will be able to avoid negative consequences. Once you get your Q1 tasks completed, you will be able to focus on other tasks. For example, if you have to submit a project at the end of the day, your complete attention should be given to that project because it is both urgent and important.

Quadrant 2: Important yet not urgent

The tasks under Q2 are important, but they are not urgent. Even though they might have a huge impact, they are not urgent. Compare Q2 to Q1, and then, you will understand the difference clearly. Typically, Q2 tasks will include the ones that have a huge impact on your long-term career or life goals. Yes, you need to allocate more time and attention to these tasks. But you seldom do it because your mind knows that the tasks in Q2 can wait. Meanwhile, you'll be focused on the tasks in other quadrants. Don't make this mistake because your long-term goals are the reasons why your short-term goals exist. For example, your health is one of the important factors, so if you don't spend enough time on it, you will regret it. Yet, when you get busy, you are unlikely to spend time on Q2 tasks. Especially, you are not obliged to answer anyone about Q2 tasks.

Quadrant 3: Urgent yet not important

The tasks under Q3 are urgent, but you don't necessarily have to spend your time in it. You can either automate or delegate the tasks to someone who can handle. These tasks are not so important, so it is okay to delegate them. These tasks often come from a third party and the tasks under Q3 will not have a direct influence on your career goals. But when you are handling Q3 tasks, you must note down the tasks that you delegate. For example, if you are working on a time-sensitive project and if the phone rings and if you attend you might get distracted. Or sometimes, it might not even be an important call. For such activities, you can assign someone. Even if it's an urgent call, you can still assign it to a person who can handle it. Through this, you will be able to manage your day!

Quadrant 4: Not important plus not urgent

The tasks under Q4 includes the tasks that need to be avoided. These tasks kill your time unnecessarily. If you don't spend ANY time on Q4 tasks, you will be able to spend more time on the tasks under Q2. By now, you'd know what Q4 tasks consist of. Anyway, they are such as watching TV, surfing the internet, playing games, and much more. So, should you eliminate Q4? Well, NO! You shouldn't. If you don't have a balanced lifestyle, you might even struggle to protect your job. The tasks in Q4 will help you whenever you take 5 minutes break or whenever you want a break from work. These tasks shouldn't even be in your mind when you are trying to be productive.

To apply the Eisenhower Matrix in your life, you must draw a table on a paper or your journal. And then, divide four columns and seven rows. Divide the rows according to the days and mention the quadrants on the columns. And then, analyze your week. But don't write down anything. Before you start the day, think and analyze again and allocate the tasks as per the matrix. If something else comes up, you must take some time to analyze the nature of the task, and then classify in the right quadrant.

Once you complete seven days, you can study the table and evaluate your effectiveness and productivity. This will not be amazing when you try it for the first time, but don't give up. Keep trying, and eventually, you will find yourself spending more time on the important and urgent tasks.

If you keep following this technique, you will be able to structure your day-to-day tasks, and it will help your success become better and better!

- 5.   Do it quickly

You come across tasks that don't need a lot of time, not even five minutes, yet you delay it. For example, cleaning after dining, sending an email, or even changing into your PJs (this is laziness). Even though these tasks don't take much time, you don't do them because you consider yourself too busy.

Your way of ignoring quick or minor tasks is by telling yourself you are busy. But the problem is whenever you delay minor tasks, it builds up into a pile, and you might have to deal with huge tasks at the end. If you don't act immediately, you will have a lot to do when you take days off. Also, if you complete the minor tasks quickly, you will be able to avoid them from piling up. There are two practices that you must know if you want to get minor tasks done.

The Two-Minute Rule is one of the practices that you must follow. If you think that the task will only take two minutes or less, you can just do it instead of putting it off. Right? So whenever you come across any minor tasks, think whether it will take longer to finish those. If they don't, why not get them done? Also, if you follow this habit throughout, you will feel that you are removing a lot of negativity and you have more time to spend on important tasks. Besides, you'll feel that you are more organized than before.

In contradiction, if you find tasks that will need more than five minutes, you must schedule a time to do it.

The second practice is to single-handle all the possible tasks. Let me describe an example, say that you've received an email and even though it requires a reply, you just delay answering it. But then, when you check it later, you would have forgotten the details on the email itself and so you have to go through all the details again. Instead of making this simple task a huge pain, you can easily get it done. The concept of single handling helps you complete the tasks. If you can see the end clearly, you must make the necessary actions. For example, you can do the dishes right away instead of putting it off for later. Likewise, there are many tasks that you have to complete immediately.

If you follow these concepts, you will be able to complete minor tasks quickly and overcome procrastination. In fact, the stress that tags along with procrastination can also be eliminated completely.

These are the simple practices that will help you beat procrastination. You don't have to worry or think low about yourself just because you are a procrastinator. We all have been procrastinators at some point in our lives. Everyone can beat procrastination if they try! Now, you have many practical tips that you can follow. You can utilize them and see if there are any changes!

You are way more powerful than you think, so ONLY you can decide whether to become a procrastinator or a productive individual!

Chapter 1 What is overthinking

Letting negativity build up in your life for a long time can bring a lot of consequences. Thankfully, we have found a way of overcoming and eliminating negativity. After overcoming and eliminating negativity, you have to deal with any consequences that may be left behind. It is easy to eliminate someone or a bad habit but the consequences caused by that habit may stay around much longer. For instance, you may decide to eliminate your behavior of sexual promiscuity after a long time. While it is a positive step in your life, the consequences associated with such behavior such as STIs may remain behind. The same case applies to negativity and negative emotions. You may finally find a way of eliminating negative energy but the consequences of negativity may remain behind.

One of the biggest consequences of negativity is overthinking. You may find that people who have suffered abuse or failure end up overthinking. Overthinking is mainly caused by negativity. The feelings of failure, unworthiness, and remorse often lead to overthinking.

Different Causes of Overthinking

There are many causes of overthinking associated with negativity. Although some people overthink in a positive way, many people overthink negatively. Some of the negative causes of overthinking include:

Low self-esteem: When a person is suffering from low self-esteem, they will often be found in isolation and deep thoughts. Suffering from low self-esteem is a consequence of letting negativity take root to the core. When you allow negative poisonous words of people get into your system, you start believing that you are worthless. Low self-esteem brings constant feelings of undeserving. Some individuals suffering from low self-esteem may contemplate suicide and often suffer from anxiety.

Fear: Another cause of overthinking is fear. Fear is brought about by thinking of the future and the past. If a person is not sure where life is headed, they will be found thinking a lot. A person who is afraid of something will keep on thinking about it. Fear causes someone to have subconscious thoughts about something. Even if you are not thinking about it actively, you will often find your subconscious mind drifting back to that instance. The best way to overcome this type of overthinking is facing your fear. Once you deal with the situation that is giving you so much fear, you will forget about it and live your life in happiness.

Shame: Shame causes overthinking to most people, even those who are emotionally strong. If you go through a shameful instance, it might be public humiliation or something that happened in a closed group you feel embarrassed. In either case, being exposed to public ridicule or being ashamed in front of family members may lead to overthinking. Although it is normal for a person to think about a shameful moment, letting your mind be focused on shameful moment's builds negativity. If you choose to focus on moments of weakness you take away your ability to focus on the future. Shame is something that will always be part of life. You must remind yourself that the shameful instance only occurred once and that it is not likely to happen. If you come to a place where you can encourage yourself to rise above shame, you build your self-esteem and build positivity. The best way to overcome shame and negativity is to always remind yourself that shameful moments don't last forever. A shameful moment may just last for a few days but it will eventually go away.

Loss: Another big cause of overthinking is a loss. When people undergo huge losses, they are often found thinking for long hours. You do not have to spend a lot of time thinking just because you have lost something or someone. You may spend a few days thinking about someone you loved so much but that should not be your ultimate life. After losing someone or something, you should remember that you have your life to pursue. The best way to deal with loss is by letting go. Accepting the reality of the situation no matter how difficult it may be. Before you come to the point of acceptance, it is not possible to let go. First, you accept that a loss has happened and that there is nothing you can do about it. After accepting, look at your life and find a way of moving on. Take your mind away from any negative thoughts and start focusing on achieving your dreams.

Failure: Failing to achieve something may also lead to overthinking. Overthinking because of failure is just a way of encouraging negative energy. All the successful people in the world have encountered failure. There is no single human being who has not made a mistake or failed to do something. Understanding that you are just human will help you overcome the pain of failure. Focusing on failure so much also stops you from pursuing other areas of life- where you might succeed. Instead of focusing on one area where you have already failed, it is better to focus on an area of life where you have a chance of succeeding.

Rejection: It is unfortunate that some people are so much drowned within the sea of worries because of being rejected. Rejection is not something you have control over. However, you have control over your emotions and thoughts. Being rejected by someone or some organization is not your fault. Stop trying to find the reason why he left you for her. The fact that someone is willing to leave your awesome life does not mean that you are weak or a bad person. When you feel dejected and worried because of rejection, you give the other person control over your life. You should not allow a person who has rejected you to control your life.

What Are The Symptoms Of Overthinking?

Overthinking is a disorder that must be corrected. If it is not handled early enough, overthinking may develop into other mental disorders that are more painful and costly. Here are the top symptoms of overthinking.

- You relive embarrassing moments in your head:

If you find yourself constantly living in an embarrassing moment, you are probably suffering from overthinking. It is okay to think about embarrassing moments but you should not relive the moment constantly. When you relive a moment, you feel like that moment is happening again right in your head. You may even show facial expressions of embarrassment. If people around you start asking why you act embarrassed, chances are that you are behaving embarrassed.

- Trouble going to sleep

The most obvious sign of overthinking is sleeping problems. People who overthink find it hard shutting the brain down. You may find yourself straining your brain to settle but nothing works. If you realize that you stay up late and wake up early, you need to examine your thinking process. You may be paying too much attention to the past or the future.

- You ask yourself a lot of questions

Do you find yourself asking what-if questions? If you ever spend your time thinking about what would have happened if you had done things the other way, you are suffering from overthinking. "What if" questions will never add anything to your life. Spending too much time wondering if you would have done things right does not make things right. Even if you make the biggest mistake of your life, you must accept that it has already happened and move on to the next phase. Spending too much time wondering what would have happened if you would have done things differently does not make things different. It only makes it hard for you to go past that specific moment.

- You try to find hidden meaning in people's words

Overthinking often leads to paranoia. You will find yourself looking at everybody with a third eye. You start looking for hidden meanings in what people say. Overthinking especially in relationships is associated with insecurity. You are unable to trust the person around you and you constantly ask investigative questions. You often find yourself drawing conclusions based on someone's words. Most people who overthink often end up starting rumors or conspiracy theories. You start imagining that there are things that happen in this world that you do not know about.

- Going over past conversations in your mind

Do you find yourself trying to redo an interview or a conversation you had before? People who overthink tend to focus on past conversations. They try making the conversation better in their mind and sometimes may be heard speaking out loud. One of the main symptoms of overthinking is speaking to yourself. Your thinking gets too loud to an extent that it cannot be contained in the mind. You relive conversations to the extent of speaking them out as if you were having the same conversation again. In most cases, people overthink when a conversation did not go right. Probably, you answered an interview question in the wrong way. Unfortunately, overthinking or rehashing a conversation does not make anything better. When you get such thoughts coming back to your mind, you must dismiss them. Being self-aware of your thought process will help you stop overthinking.

- Lack of concentration

People who overthink are often found lost in another world. If you are constantly found lost in your thoughts and unaware of what is happening around you, you are probably overthinking. When you overthink, your mind is transported to another world. You do not pay attention to what you are doing and in most cases; you may run into an accident. If you realize that people often have to tap your shoulder for attention or call your name out a loud, you have to start examining your thinking process. At this stage, your thought process has been corrupt to such an extent that you no longer live in the real world. Most of your days are spent in another world reliving moments from the past

- You are always worried

Worries are as a result of overthinking. When a person overthinks, he/she keeps on wondering what if this and that may happen. These thoughts may focus on the future or the past. When a person is thinking about the past, he/she will worry about the consequences of the choices they made in the past. You will find yourself asking questions like; what if I was wrong? On the other hand, people may also think about the future. What if such things happen in the future? Thinking about the future and the past will only give you unnecessary worries. Things that have already happened cannot be redone. The future is something abstract. Until you understand that the future only exists in your mind, you will keep on wasting a lot of time thinking about tomorrow. You should always remind yourself that life is good today and that you should enjoy it.

How To Control Overthinking

You need to find a way of controlling your thoughts. Controlling your thoughts is not easy especially after going through an embarrassing moment. However, you need to control your thinking for your own good. There are many ways to control your thinking.

Be aware of your thoughts: Try practicing self-awareness if you find yourself constantly drifting to another world. When you are aware of your thoughts, you will interrupt them and stop thinking in the same direction. Unfortunately, most people who suffer from overthinking disorder do not even recognize that they are overthinking. When a person is in a state of thinking, the thoughts keep on piling up in a chain process, with one leading to another.

To enhance your awareness, start practicing self-awareness in your daily life. A practical exercise includes reflecting on your thought process after every few minutes. Ask yourself what you have been thinking about the last 1 hour or 30 minutes. You may even set reminders on your phone to help you check your thought process after a few minutes. The reminder will constantly get you out of your negative thoughts and set you on the right path again. Self-awareness should help you forgo thinking and start focusing on your life at the moment.

- Choose the things you want to think about

If you realize that overthinking is always occupying your mind, find something different to think about. This will help you deal with the negative thoughts that go through your head. You may decide to think about the most beautiful things in your life. If you have someone you love, you may choose to think about their beauty and everything good they add to your life. Finding a different focal point for your thoughts will help you control your thought process.

In essence, the two basic ways of controlling your thinking are interrupting your thought process and focusing on a different thinking direction. Since overthinking is about negativity in most cases, you need to interrupt the continuous flow of negative thoughts in your head. Stop any thought that does not lead to productivity through self-awareness and setting reminders. This will prohibit you from going deep into the world of negativity. Once you interrupt the thought process from negativity, focus it on beauty. Look at your life and think about things that are beautiful, lovely and attractive. Life has both positive and negative sides. Although the mind always wants to focus on simple mistakes and negative events, you are the one to control the negativity. You may train your mind to start thinking positively and concentrate on positivity at all times. Once you can stop your thoughts and redirect them, you completely gain control over your thinking and as a result, manage to control overthinking.

How To Stop Overthinking

It is one thing to control overthinking but a different story entirely to stop it. Controlling overthinking entails interrupting and disrupting the overthinking process. You may use reminders and other thoughts to interrupt your mind and control overthinking. However, most often than not, people who try disrupting the thinking process without addressing the root cause often drift back into their thoughts. To stop overthinking, you need to address the cause from the root. You need to examine the cause of your thoughts and deal with it. Controlling overthinking only deals with the symptoms, but stopping overthinking deals with the root cause. Here is a simple step by step process to help you stop overthinking.

Step 1: Find the root cause: The first thing you need to do is find the root of your thinking. As soon as you notice that there are symptoms of overthinking showing up in your life, examine your thought process to determine what you are constantly thinking about. In most cases, you will find that you think because of worry or fear. If you are afraid or worried about something happening, you will spend a lot of time thinking. The positive side of overthinking is usually due to anticipation. Even anticipation of good things should not occupy your mind. You must deal with all these factors to totally stop overthinking about things that may or may not happen.

Step 2: Accept the situation: You need to accept the situation that has led to your fears and worries. You need to accept that this has already happened and that there is nothing you can do about it. However, if there is something you can do about it to make it better, take action immediately. Taking action to stop something bad from happening will also alleviate thinking. Constantly thinking about something that already happened or is about to happen does not help. If it is something that has already happened, except that it is done. If it something that is yet to happen, you can take action about it. Taking action does not necessarily mean stopping it from happening but reducing consequences if possible. Think about your worries and examine the ones you can salvage. If there is nothing you can salvage, stop thinking about it and take action.

Step 3: Face your fears and address your worries: Overthinking is null thinking process that does not result in any solution. However, you need to stand up to your fears if you want to stop thinking about it. The first thing you should do after examining the cause of your worries is to ask yourself what you can do about it. In the case of fear, you only have an option of facing it. Facing your fears entails preparing yourself to stand for your rights and being ready for the consequences of your mistakes. Some of the ways to face your fears include accepting punishment, offering an apology, grieving in terms of loss among others. If you have been overthinking because of a mistake you did at the office, you may choose to face the fear by offering an apology and being ready to take the consequences. One of the things you must constantly keep in your mind is that life cannot be determined by one instance. Even when you lose a job, always remember that there is another option for you. You should be ready to face the consequences of every situation knowing that it's just a moment in life. That moment does not stop life from moving on any grounds.

Step 4: Move on: The other big cause of fear is staying in the past. Whatever happened has already happened and thinking about it does not take it way. In fact, spending too much time thinking about it only brings pain. People who have been heartbroken in relationships tend to spend too much time thinking about the past. You must find a way of dealing with such thoughts. The thoughts of having a relationship with a person who has already rejected you only bring pain. To completely stop the overthinking process, move on.

Moving on means that you open a new chapter in life. If you are overthinking because you lost a job, open a new chapter by starting a business or looking for another job. If it is due to a broken relationship, move on to another relationship. If it is due to the loss of life of a friend, accept the realities and move on. Moving on means that you choose to focus your mind on something else that gives you joy. One of the best tactics of controlling your thought process is finding something else that keeps you busy. Moving on gives you the chance to think objectively. When you are still attached to someone or something, it is hard to think soberly. However, when you move on, you start seeing the positives and negatives of the matter clearly.

You Have Trouble Getting To Sleep

One of the biggest problems associated with overthinking is lack of sleep. If you can manage to deal with the problem of overthinking, getting sleep should not be a big problem. However, before you completely eliminate the overthinking, you need to start dealing with your sleep problems. Lack of sleep often results in fatigue and mood swings.

When you lack good sleep, you are easily irritable and less productive at work. To deal with sleep problems due to overthinking you can:

- Count sheep

Counting sheep is a technique used to gain concentration. Psychologically, most people cannot think about other things when counting something. Counting needs your full attention, otherwise, you will find yourself loosing track. It does not have to be sheep you are counting but rather anything that will take the mind off your thoughts. When you go to bed, imagine yourself on a farm of sheep and start counting them on by one. Count in sets of ten and start over until you reach a hundred. Closing your eyes and counting sheep will help you gain sleep even before you reach the 100 marks. It is so easy to get sleep when you count sheep or anything else.

- II) Meditation

Although counting sheep is a form of meditation too, you may choose to meditate using the conventional meditation styles. The best form of meditation is mindfulness. If you find yourself losing sleep and concentration, try mindfulness.

Chapter 2 Differences between overthinking and anxiety

You make progress by setting four types of intention

- power

- perspective

- productivity

- play

You'll need to set these four intentions before the start of each week to make sure your focus is on progress and moving forward.

When I set my intentions each week, I like to break them down into really simple steps. It only takes me five to ten minutes on a Sunday to get my intentions mapped out, so I am ready for the week ahead. There really is no excuse for not doing this.

When you choose your intentions, you need to pick something simple and effective (not necessarily easy, mind you). 'Simple' gets it done – 'complicated' gives you an excuse to procrastinate).

These intentions help keep the train moving forwards, they also act as reminders of your destination at the stops and help you make good choices rather than not so good ones.

POWER

- This is your personal power that comes from within yourself. Some people think of this as their "'inner warrior'" or sometimes '#beastmode' or whatever you choose that represents a strong, fit, energetic and powerful version of you.

Power provides your confidence in your own abilities, your day-to-day energy and enthusiasm. It's also your physical ability to move better, feel stronger and challenge yourself consistently. This is really important, because your confidence and energy are going to be a huge factor in whether or not you're going to move forward and challenge yourself week to week.

Confidence and energy (in my opinion) are best built with good exercise and a good eating routine. It has become a ritual I have followed for many years.

EXAMPLES OF POWER INTENTIONS

Have a go at setting some power intentions yourself for the next week. This is something you intend to do in the next seven days that will help you progress in your personal power (confidence and energy).

Here are some examples help you...

- 'do some exercise six days this week'

'burn more calories each day - track via 'Fitbit'

'drink a greens drink daily upon waking'

'join Grant's fitness class Tue and Thurs'

Don't worry if you're not 100% sure you've picked the right thing, just pick something that would help you move forwards this coming week for now and see what happens. I'll ask you to do a proper weekly plan soon, and you can refine your ideas then.

Do you see the benefits to this technique? It's a simple intention that, once written down, will give you the extra motivation you need to move you forward and then you likely will achieve it by the end of the week.

It doesn't have to be too fancy or hard. And you can use the same intention over and over as long as it's making you actually DO IT and get some progress out of it. If you want to use it until you feel you need a new one, that's fine. As long as you're still progressing and feel it's challenging you, then keep doing it!

A frequent power intention of mine is "get stronger and faster this week."' Now, I don't fully know that I will, but I damn sure will try. I track my workouts each week for reps/weight/time, etc., so I know that, to get better, I need to be faster or stronger than last week to be sure I've progressed and hit my intention.

I'll sometimes seek out some accountability from a coach or friend when it comes to workouts.

If you don't hit the intention, remember not to dwell on it. Instead, seek out the lesson in why things didn't go to plan. Maybe you weren't rested enough. Maybe you hadn't eaten enough food. Maybe you were distracted with some overwhelming thoughts in your head. Whatever it is, you need to ask yourself "why have I not hit that intention this 'week? " and be honest with yourself. (Once I've explained all four Ps, I'll explain more of what happens if you don't hit an intention).

PERSPECTIVE

- Perspective is everything when it comes to becoming more calm and controlled – and you want to be that, right? Less overthinking, more in control of our choices and more peaceful with your decisions.

Your perspective is either going to cause you immense pain – or absolute pride and pleasure. Controlling your perspective is a bit like being able to "'look on the bright side". How you see (i.e. make sense of) things makes a dramatic difference to your life. Of course, you have your beliefs, or standards, and sometimes they won't change, but your perspective always can.

Ever been furious with someone then talked it out, got their take on the matter, understood them fully, then thought to yourself "Ah, I understand now from their point of view. It makes it so much easier for us both now."

That is perspective!

And it's so powerful.

So, how do you set your perspective intention for the next seven days? Just like power, You make simple and worthwhile statements to aim for.

EXAMPLES OF PERSPECTIVE INTENTIONS

Have a go at setting some perspective intentions for the week.

Here are some examples to help you…

- 'read 15 minutes of the mindset book daily'

'watch a daily TED Talk on YouTube'

'sit and relax on my own for 10 minutes daily'

'have a proper conversation with the Mrs about our views'

'watch daily, Luke John Harrison's 'Daily Boom'

…snuck that last one in there, ha ha. :-)

But you get my point, right?

Your perspective intention is something simple you can do to help you see things clearer, for example, improve your outlook, mindset and calmness. It's sometimes referred to nowadays as 'mindfulness' and, just like training in the gym, it takes time and effort to see results in this area too.

Simply having some time on your own, to be with your thoughts and see what comes your way, is very profound.

You could call this 'meditation', but I prefer 'relaxation' over 'meditation'. It seems easier to do for most people. It's crucial to relax to gain perspective of what's truly important to you.

You may be surprised at what ten minutes of quiet time will do towards figuring out a fresh perspective.

If you want to strengthen your perspective muscle, listen to motivational speakers and coaches every morning upon waking. There are plenty of podcasts, TED talks, and YouTube videos to pick from.

PRODUCTIVITY

- Productivity relates to your financial abundance, which you can progress, yes?

If you're in some sort of business, you're aware that businesses live and die on sales. So, doesn't it make sense to get better at selling?

If you've got a job, how about learning a new skill or getting a new qualification to enable you to get that promotion you wanted, and the pay rise to boot?

Your productivity intention looks at what you can do to make yourself more valuable.

If you were to be more financially stable and abundant, do you think it would calm your overthinking a little, leaving you to focus on the simple changes you need to make to improve your situation?

Of course it would. Money lubricates your life.

It helps you do nice things for yourself and others. Remember, you're on the "I'm worth it" train, where you're worth nice things.

It also enables you to genuinely help more people, because you're less worried and distracted about the finances and more focused on building strong relationships and genuinely helping people.

Ask yourself, "is this financial position I'm in now, what I want for the rest of my life?" It should spark some emotion. If the answer's 'no', you need to focus on some ways of progressing your income.

So how?

Well, an intention for this side of things could be "network with 'said' business this week" to improve your relationships with people. It could be something like "study leadership book or sales video 20 minutes daily." It could be "study money book 10 pages daily'." It could be "make five sales." It could be "find out more about further opportunities within the company you work for", or even studying "workplace morale building" So, many options, what speaks to you? What do you need to learn the most?

If you know how to make sales already, write the intention to get it done, like "make five sales this week through x, y, z." This is progress, is it not? And, by the way, yes you can study money – a great money book is Stuart Wilde's 'The Trick To Money Is Having Some'.

It doesn't take a genius to know you need to grow and progress when it comes to financial abundance and your professional life.

And, to do that, you guessed it, you need to set an INTENTION for the next seven days.

HOW TO SET A PRODUCTIVITY INTENTION

Have a go at setting some productivity intentions for the coming week.

Here are some examples to help you.

- 'make three sales this week for online program'

'study the marketing book, 10 pages each day'

'write five pages of your book each day'

By the way, all intentions are strengthened when you add numbers to them, otherwise they can be a bit casual and irrelevant. Numbers help with making your intention trackable and more fun to achieve, for example being five pages ahead, £200 richer, 20 seconds faster, two reps stronger, would feel pretty good, yes?

You get the point, start low, then gradually build those numbers to challenge yourself, :-).

And, finally, your last P.

PLAY

- This is a weird one for some folks. But have a think for a moment. How many people simply don't plan any play time. It's quite a shock when you stop and reflect on that. You seem to feel 'too busy' and 'don't have time' for rest and relaxation.

Oh man, you need to make time to have some shut off time, time to recharge, especially if you want to make progress.

Even a finely tuned, powerful Formula One car has to pull into the pits for a new set of tyres. It's the same for you, my friend.

For your play intention, pick something that's going take you away from the pressures of life and the worries of everything.

This could be something fun, exciting, and stimulating – something that makes you feel truly alive. It could be something peaceful and restful – something that gives you some breathing space and a break from the constant hustle and bustle of modern life. (I consciously slot in time each week to see my best mate for lunch and play some video games – I call it #BromanceFriday :-) – and it happens because I write a play intention for it).

You may experience some resistance towards planning your play time, especially if you've not done it for a while, but it's vitally important for you to progress in all areas of life. It keeps your "I'm worth it" train in top-notch condition.

Some rest and relaxation works wonders. It helps you gain perspective and clarity and relaxes your nervous system. Even something simple like laughing produces the right hormones for your body to remind itself how rewarding enjoying yourself really is.

This intention could involve alone time or time connecting with others, date night, family time, friend gatherings or even just you and your X-box having a night in.

HOW TO SET A PLAY INTENTION

Have a go at setting some play intentions for the week.

Here are some examples to help you...

'One hour alone X-box time Sunday pm'

'Warwick dinner and games Friday lunch'

'Tuesday night lads' board game night'

'Cinema date with lady friend on Thursday'

Play time could be literally anything. Let your mind run riot – especially if you feel life has become nothing more than the daily grind.

What I would say is that this should probably be the easiest intention to set. Remember what you used to enjoy doing, but then 'life' got in the way? Revisit that activity and feel once again the joy that it used to bring you.

As always, keep it simple and write it down!

Keep these intentions handy because you'll be planning the next day very shortly. There's an example to show you how on the next page.

HOW TO SET GOOD INTENTIONS

- Let's break this down super simple in case you're stuck.

What's important to you? I imagine it's to feel like you're getting somewhere? Like you're on track, yes?

And you probably know eating some more vegetables this week and getting a few gym sessions, or brisk walks in the fresh air would help you to feel better, yes?

You probably know studying five pages of that book you heard was great would probably do you good.

I imagine you've been following someone on social media who you'd like to work or connect with on a deeper level at some point. Send them a message to interact with them.

Perhaps setting a date night with your partner would probably make you both feel better, yes?

Single? Ask someone who you quite fancy for a coffee. If they say no, just accept it and move onto the next, you're worth it :-).

Make sure you have not committed to achieving "all the things."

Once you have a list of potential activities for all four Ps, you need to choose the ones you are going to make progress towards.

TASK: CHOOSE YOUR INTENTIONS FOR THIS WEEK

- Now you know how progress works, it's time to choose your four intentions for the coming week.

Pick your favourite option for each of the Ps and set it to be your intention for the week.

Keep it simple, don't commit to doing too much. Remember, it's easy to use complexity as an excuse.

Remember, willpower is finite. You're going to hit a point where you think "I really can't be bothered today." And the reason you must be bothered is that willpower will only go so far. You have to choose long term commitment over feeling in the moment to really get shit done.

Think back to a time when you gave up in the past – did you just not feel like it or did something genuinely get in the way?

Sometimes you may slip and not achieve an intention. That's ok, LEARN FROM IT!

Be aware though that most "reasons" are bullshit and it's these sorts of flimsy "reasons" that keep you miserable.

You're used to being comfortable and having certainty in your life. Even procrastinating gives you certainty, because you just do the things you're used to.

But, right now, you do not want to stay miserable, right?

If you don't set intentions and have a plan before the week comes, you will tend to fill your time with unhelpful or neutral stuff.

When you don't have a plan, or set intentions, you're more likely to procrastinate, right? We've discovered this. So, let me just remind you of how stupid this can get. This is a story is about Olympic standard time-wasting.

THE THREE SHITS STORY

Years back, when I was a plumber, often boredom used to set in. You've probably noticed how tempting it is to do stupid stuff when you're bored, hence, why many folk create drama, or go back to an ex when they don't want to, or constantly give in to bingeing on food or alcohol.

One day, me and my two pals had finished our plumbing in a bathroom suite in an empty house early, which meant we had a few hours to kill.

We finished our baits (lunches) and we all needed the toilet. It was a very bored me, that piped up with

"Hey lads, I know why don't we all have a shit in the toilet? But not flush after each other and see who can cope with it?" They laughed hysterically, then realised I was serious...

Yup, I have no fucking idea to this day why I thought why the three shits challenge was a good idea, but, still, they actually agreed.

That begged the question... 'Who goes first?' So, we all drew straws and who got the short straw? Yours truly...

So, my mate goes in, does his business and doesn't flush. My other mate goes on top (literally), then comes out practically gagging...

Then I enter to have a shit, on top of a shit, on top of a shit...

There I was, sitting down, wretching, gagging, taking half breaths because of the smell of shit... I finish, then flush, then hurriedly leave to be sick.

Moral of the story? Boredom makes you do stupid things. Make yourself less bored by setting intentions.

- A gentle reminder for you, and I can't re iterate enough how powerful this is, the more consistently you meet your intentions, the better your results.

I've done 'Daily Boom' videos now for over three years (as of writing this book) and people know me because of that consistency.

I can help hundreds of people and get new clients because of my consistency in sharing these short videos. I need to do that to grow my business and meet my productivity intentions.

For you, it doesn't have to be daily videos. You choose something simple you can do consistently that serves you and others. I promise you, you will reap you benefits in the long run, more than you may be able to see right now.

Three years ago I never dreamed I'd be writing a book, but I credit 80% plus of my success to my daily consistent videos; I know I have ideas worth sharing. You must have consistency to be a success.

Think of it as a little bit more effort, but never a chore.

Sometimes putting in all the effort can seem a chore when you're not seeing results, but don't worry, it takes time in whatever you're striving for. It will happen for you if you're consistent —

like making all those mortgage payments for 25 years to own your own home.

HOW TO KEEP MEETING YOUR INTENTIONS

This may seem a little scary at first, but you'll read a story shortly in the coming pages about my porn addiction and how telling people helped me overcome and achieve more.

No one wants to look like a failure, so, telling others will help and hold you accountable. You will not want to lose face and will keep meeting your intentions. Being accountable is key; remember, it's what moves you towards more progress!

Remember to plan the activities you need to meet your intentions in your daily planner sheet (Download my worked example to see what you need to do in detail.)

Why not see if a friend will join the progress train with you? Explain how it works and ask them to climb aboard! It's so much easier to progress when you're around people on the same journey as you.

Chapter 3 Symptoms of overthinking

When I am in San Francisco, I like to go to a café in Japan Town. It's a quiet, dark little café with an excellent mocha latte and unreliable internet that prevents me from getting too distracted from the book I'm reading – or writing. But is good enough to search for the basics in Google. I usually spend a couple of hours there, and then I go to a nearby grocery store to buy some sushi makis for lunch. After a few occasions, I discovered that I get always the same things. One plate of tuna makis and one of salmon makis.

The thing is, I don't really like tuna that much. I like salmon much more. Still, for the sake of variety I buy both of them instead of buying only salmon makis. If I had to choose only one plate, I'd choose the salmon. If I went to eat lunch twice choosing only one plate, I'd choose salmon both times. Why do I end up buying tuna, then?

For the sake of variety? What variety? Why is variety even better? Do I buy them because this is how I show appreciation for salmon makis? If I only had salmon makis, all of them would be the same, established on a relatively low place my personal scale of worth. However, having only half salmon makis makes them more valuable. You may wonder, "Okay, salmon makis, got it, but where are you heading with this crazy brainstorm?"

Let me get to the point. Having this seemingly useless mental chatter on my way back to the café after lunch made me realize something.

Some of the mental chatter and clutter is necessary to make you satisfied. If you are only thinking about valuable information, you're always on the point, none of your thoughts would be truly valuable. Some unimportant mental chatter gives true value for the good thoughts. You appreciate good thoughts more because they are more scarce, and pop out in your nonsensical mental chatter.

Does the nonsense make you feel weird sometimes? Sure it does. But this weirdness is also part of you. Searching for a slightly less wrong answer through your emotional memory arsenal is not a bad thing. Without thinking about something, you won't find answers. That way you'll accept others' "truth" that will inevitably feel foreign, make you feel uncomfortable and turn on your brain-munching bug of overthinking.

Let me clarify it now.

This kind of inner chatter is the purest, most innocent instinctive voice of yours. This voice has a childish curiosity, a willingness to discover and understand the world for your benefit, not to mess your life up. If you want a visual picture about it, this voice is the proverbial angel on your right shoulder. It's the voice of your true personality, part of those little quirks and perks that make you you. This relentless pure chatter will give birth to some great ideas that take you forward instead of holding you back.

You know how can you distinguish "helpful mental chatter" from that compulsory feeling of overthinking? Helpful mental chatter is followed by action. Overthinking serves mostly to avoid taking action.

There's a weird paradox in our overthinking system. We overthink because if something is not complicated, or doesn't seem challenging enough, we attach little value to it. It's not worthy of action. As soon as we overcomplicate it, we fail taking action, because it then scares us.

Some people know what they are supposed to do, but they simply don't act. Others get stuck in analysis paralysis to avoid failure and pain. However, avoiding pain and failure is not helpful. It fosters people from the chance to learn. Not knowing the future, a failure today can become a great success tomorrow, if you let it.

Ditch the analysis paralysis, and make decisions instead. Whatever decision you make will bring you somewhere. It can be a place for success or a place to learn. Yet, failing to make a decision means you failed to learn and grow. Now and then you'll hit proverbial forks in the road. When this happens, you may think that you have two options, going left or going right. The Minimalists, Joshua Fields Millburn and Ryan Nicodemus, argue that you have not two but four choices when it comes to an existential crossroads.

The first option is what they call "the right path". This is the path of an obvious right decision. There are no questions related to this road. It is like Broadway, surrounded by palm trees, illuminated, and fireworks sparking all the way around. These are choices like, "Should I kill my banker for mismanaging my money or shall I solve this issue peacefully within the borders of the law?" Obviously, the first option is a no-no.

The other side of the obvious choices is called "the wrong path". Choices here are blatantly wrong. If you have a little reason, conscience or sensibility, you avoid these routes. Sometimes they may seem quite tempting, like telling your annoying boss that, "She's an ugly witch with serious sociopath manners, it's no wonder she doesn't have a husband." Taking revenge on her in such a manner is a very attractive option, but you and I both know that you're much better than that.

The Minimalists call the third type of choice one can make "the left path". In many cases one path seems right but so does the other. Maybe you cannot tell which path is the better one. Maybe one would be good short term, the other long term. Like the translation offer I once received, X dollars advance plus ten percent royalty, or no advance but twenty percent royalty. Clearly, for the short term the first option sounded more tempting. Who cares about a five-year-length reward when she can spend the earnings today? In these cases the best choice is to collect all the pros and cons of today for both options. Why today? Because who knows what tomorrow brings. You can't know what your future self will wish. If you picked right, good job. If you picked wrong, learn from it. I picked the second option, by the way, the long term twenty percent. Why? Based on my needs of today, I didn't need quick money, fortunately. Since I didn't know how I would stand financially in five years, that twenty percent secure savings gives me peace of mind. In my case, long term investment was a pro of today.

The fourth choice is to make no choice at all. When we look at two unknown possibilities, we often freeze and start overthinking them, get into analysis paralysis to avoid taking action and failure. Not making a decision is also a decision, but it is the worst kind. It will keep you stuck.

- Why You Shouldn't Worry About Your Decisions Too Much

I could answer this hypothesis with a simple cliché answer, like you are just small dust in the endless eternity of the universe. Your decisions don't usually make any significant change to the big picture, so don't take yourself so seriously. Well, if I was looking for an answer, and read a book that served me with something I just said, I'd be very grateful, because I knew with what to light my first fire come winter.

Here is another, less cliché answer that might actually help your decision-making mind monster. Decisions that we have to make each day are connected to one single frame of time, our future.

As a matter of fact, there is no other species on earth that anticipates future events like we humans do. Squirrels may save nuts for winter, migratory birds might fly south, but their squirrel and bird brains don't construct their futures like ours do. They are simple, driven by basic instinct, and sensing a decrease in temperature they know that it is time to do what they have coded in their nature. They put together present events (I feel cold) with past events (last time I stayed here for too long when it was cold, I almost froze) to "predict" a possible consequence for the future. Their brain doesn't jump to these conclusions based on conscious thoughts, only purely instinctual ones. Daniel Gilbert in his bestselling book, Stumbling On Happiness calls this kind of predictions "nexting". What is nexting? It's an alternative made-up word by him to refer to predictions such as the squirrel's nut scavenging habits. Decisions like that are short-term decisions triggered by the here and now. They are not far-reaching predictions like stock market change, the next dominant musical or painting style, or Taylor Swift's next boyfriend. Nexting is a chain of decision-making in the present moment.

Every moment you make a nexting type of decision. Now, for example you're reading my lines nexting about where this thought about nexting is going. It is nexting when you take your umbrella instinctively when you see clouds outside. Nexting is completing a sentence that starts with "my heart will" with "go on". If we, humans could only do nexting, we wouldn't be any different than our canary in the cage. The canary doesn't have any sense about the future, it just peacefully twitters, swinging on its little swing. When it's hungry, he squeaks loudly because it knows that food will follow. The reflex of the bird's brain is built upon the angry owner's lack of patience.

We are different. An unprecedented growth doubled the size of the brain of our ancestors, making the one-and-a-quarter-pound brain of the Homo habilis a nearly three-pound brain of the Homo sapiens. Breaking down this growth to different areas, a disproportionate growth affected a certain area of the brain that we call the frontal lobe. This part of the brain, as you might have guessed from its name, is positioned above the eyes, in the front of the skull. (C. A. Banyas, "Evolution and Phylogenetic History of the Frontal Lobes", pg. 83-106)

In the 1800s psychologists and neurologists assumed that the frontal lobe was a good-for-nothing part of the brain which if gets injured, nothing really changes in a person's behavior. Later, in the early 1900s, their opinion slightly changed. Following some experiments made on monkeys, they observed that lobotomizing them (chemically or mechanically destroying some parts of the frontal lobe) they became much calmer afterwards. The animals that were previously outraged if their food was withheld now patiently waited for their portion. A Portuguese physician,

António Egas Moniz, tried the method on human patients in the mid 1900s to treat anxiety and depression. They experienced the same effect as the monkeys. They felt much calmer. (D. Gilbert, "Stumbling on Happiness", pg. 13-14.)

As a matter of fact, they were very calm, like not having any worry in the world. The breakthrough discovery of the next decades regarding the damage to the frontal lobe stated that people lost their ability to think about the future. Patients with frontal lobe damage seemed unchanged as long as they didn't have to make any predictions about the future, they didn't have to plan. What's common in planning and anxiety? They are both future-related. Scientists today admit that humans without a healthy frontal lobe are like canaries, trapped in the eternal present, unable to "consider the self's extended existence throughout time." (Gilbert, pg. 15.)

The frontal lobe, the youngest part of our brain, makes long-term planning happen. Long-term plans are those that require our attention to choose one of the four types of decisions we can make (preferably number one and three, choosing the right thing or the left thing). I also stated that making these long term decisions shouldn't worry us too much – and not because we're just dust in the wind.

It is because we don't know our future selves.

Your future self is like an ungrateful child. It doesn't matter how much you struggle making the best possible decisions for future you, it won't be enough. Whatever you consider the best for your future self today, in a few years it will seem rather odd or dull. And that's good. It means you grew. You have a wider perspective and you are less wrong about things than you were a few years before.

What I say here doesn't mean you shouldn't choose the best option possible your today's mind can conceive for your future self, but don't overthink it. Take it easy, because chances are that your future self "will know it better" anyway. Do you ever recall some opinions you had a while ago that today seem totally nutty? Yes, that's your current self trashing your past self, who, guess what, made the best decision you could make at that moment.

I was a late bloomer. I truly believed that my first relationship would be the last and we'd always be together, having a vegetable garden and dogs. When we broke up I thought I'd never love again. With my second girlfriend I thought that this love was not how love was supposed to look like, like there was a standard for love. I was full of weird thoughts and decisions that, I thought then, served my best interests. Today I can only laugh about them. When my first girlfriend broke up with me, I was devastated. I decided to believe that I'd never be okay again –I was ever wrong.

I remember how frozen, broken and depressed I was when I decided to break up with my second girlfriend. I thought the sorrow would never cease and I would never be happy. Wrong again. Those decisions that were so painful and difficult to my past self are the best things that ever happened to my present self. The rule works the other way around, as well. Present tragedies can turn into future successes.

Put that frontal lobe to work on the best future you can conceive today, but don't overestimate its decision's effect on your long-term life. Don't overload your mind with worries.

Don't try to foresee what your future self will want. Don't overthink your options. Use the best of whatever you have now, and make a choice based on those values. Your future self may or may not like your choices of today, but your heart in present will be at peace. That's the only thing you can aim to control.

Chapter 4 How to stop negative thinking

In this context, we take the view that emotions are a form of energy created by the body to communicate to you how your overall body status is and it is advisable that you allow this energy to dissipate. When the body status is calm and relaxes, you will feel energized, happy and excited. This positive energy will be expressed by tears of joy, eagerness and lengthened the period of patience. On the other hand, when your body status is feeling threatened and unease you are going to express that energy in the form of fear, anger, and impatience. In this manner, emotional intelligence is about learning to acknowledge your emotions and finding a way to safely release them rather than blocking them. Most individuals wrongly think that negative emotions are unwanted when in real sense, they are part of the human experience and what is required is to find a safe way to release that energy without harming others.

Correspondingly, being highly sensitive is not a form of weakness. On the contrary, it is the society that is becoming numb to empathy and becoming dysfunctional to allowing expression of all emotions. There is nothing wrong with expressing your authentic emotions. It is unfortunate that the society castigates people that express their real emotions and celebrates those that bottle up emotions in a misguided effort to create standardized society. Human behavior is dynamic and it cannot be standardized but we can build a shared spectrum of what is ideal and what is not. Against this understanding, do not blame yourself as being a mess or easily irked because it is the society that is pushing for suppressing of authentic feelings. However, it is important that you find a safe way to defuse negative emotions to avoid creating fear and avoidance from people around you.

"Maintain calmness even when you have a thousand reasons not to be"

Even though this quote seems to contradict the first quote, it is not. While it is vital to manifest your emotions, both positive and negative, it is important to take time before fully expressing negative emotions. For positive emotions, it might be excusable to act impulsively but it is still advisable to exercise restraint. Remember that within the context of emotional intelligence it is critical to consider how others feel. Your excitement could be happening at a time when one of your colleagues has been sacked or going through a divorce. With this understanding, learning to slow down your reaction can help improve your emotional intelligence. Emotions are impulsively and you will have to learn to anticipate certain emotions to enhance the manner that you react to them.

"Emotional health affects your self-esteem"

It is critical that you learn to diagnose yourself because your emotional state affects your self-esteem levels. By identifying what is troubling you, it will enable you to read more about the trigger and how to handle it before it fully manifests. For emphasis, most individuals tend to overlook the fact that positive emotions can also adversely impact your personality. For instance, if you are highly excitable there are chances that you are likely to overlook finer details of anything and may have difficulties planning for the long-term. In other terms, excessively manifesting positive emotions can make you highly vulnerable to the environmental factors as any significant change may make it difficult for you to recover.

Equally important is that part of your self-esteem constitutes the self-assurance that you can navigate any situation. For this reason, it is critical that you experience or become aware of both negative and positive emotions. As expected, building the ability to recognize your emotional health and attend to it happens over time with guidance and commitment. Once you master the art of diagnosing and fixing your emotional health, then your levels of self-esteem will increase, as you are likely to navigate any situation. Simply put, negative emotional health will lower your self-esteem levels. One of the ways of diagnosing yourself is through meditation and learning to extricate yourself from your thoughts to develop an independent view of the situation.

"Life is an active process"

Through acknowledging that life is an active process, you are recognizing that human behavior and actions are dynamic.

Human behavior is both predictable and uncertain. What differentiates an emotionally stable person from a highly sensitive individual is their emotional intelligence levels. Individuals regarded as emotionally stable exhibit the desired ability to express both negative and positive emotions in an acceptable manner through training or experience. The emphasis is on the degree of reacting to emotions and that all emotions should be expressed. Locking up emotions is counterproductive as at one point you will experience an emotional outburst or get overwhelmed by the emotions and make an irrational and sometimes fatal decision. You should remember that bottling up emotions could be a danger not only to you but to those around including physical systems if you work in critical installations.

Since life is an active process, you should accept that learning would not stop. There will be new techniques and suggestions that are new to you and it will require mentorship and training to master them. All these realizations encourage us to try learning about emotional intelligence since life is an active process and there are high chances of improving our emotional intelligence. From the feedback, you gather about the way you react to particular situations, you should seek ways to acknowledge and manage the specific reaction. Adjusting your emotional intelligence level to desirable levels are informed by the fact the human mind and emotional state can be altered. These realizations are the core pillars of advancing emotional intelligence as a concept to be learned, internalized and operationalized.

For example, remember when you used to cry when left alone as a child but as you grew up you started cherishing freedom. As a toddler, your mind and exposure had only assured you that you could only be safe around your parents or caregiver. The extrication of the caregiver from your life temporarily generated uncertainty and unfamiliarity. You expressed the negative emotions by crying continuously. However, as you grew you learned to convert the absence of caregivers in your life temporarily as an opportunity to explore yourself and your environment. The temporary freedom granted you an opportunity to express positive emotions in the form of feeling energized, playful, and confident. What learn from this simple illustration is that life is an active process and we express certain emotions based on our understanding of our self and the immediate environment. Emotional intelligence can be learned by manipulating the internal and external factors that make us react in a specific manner.

"Through enlarging the acknowledgment spectrum, your emotional intelligence begins to grow"

Through this statement, we learned that loosening up and being open-minded up can lessen the need to bottle up emotions as well as increasing chances of manifesting negative emotions. As indicated earlier, stereotypes and other prejudices predispose you to make premature judgments that compromise empathy in interactions. Furthermore, sustaining prejudices requires significant mental while denying you numerous opportunities to recognize positive emotions. At an individual level, lack of being open-minded may use up your physical and mental energy as you try to force a conclusion where it should not suffice. Therefore, learning to allow a large degree of freedom before concluding allows you more options some of which are likely to lead to a decreased need to manifest negative emotions.

Additionally, being open-minded increases empathy quality in conversations. Think of trying to have a conversation with a divorcee as having preformed opinion that divorcees entered marriage institution before adequately courting. While having the conversation with the divorcee, your mind will always extrapolate your opinions from the premise that divorcees enter marriage union before adequately knowing each other well. In essence, you are not actively listening to the individual you are talking to because you have allowed the little knowledge you have to become the ultimate knowledge. Some educationists argue that the most overlooked aspect of learning is the ability to unlearn which most people struggle with.

"Meditation is not necessarily emotional intelligence but it can be a critical tool for emotional intelligence"

Even though meditation has numerous benefits, it is not necessarily emotional intelligence. The importance of meditation is that it can significantly increase the self-awareness of an individual. As seen earlier, self-awareness is a critical plank of emotional intelligence. Without individual learning to understand itself and its shortcomings, there is little motivation to seek help and commit to the advice and training provided thereafter. In the initial stages of improving an individual's emotional intelligence, meditation is a valuable tool. Meditation can be a form of self-feedback and it can also be used as a means for an individual to remove himself from the self to form an alternate view of everything. However, if a person is not eased with meditation the person should not be forced to undertake it.

"Develop healthy boundaries and enforce them"

While a lot has been presented on how to be considerate of others and how to adjust your individual desires to attain balance with others, there is a need for setting boundaries. You can still specify and enforce limits of what you can absorb and what you can manifest. Remember that while adjusting yourself to listen and empathize with others, they also have a moral duty to understand and accept you. Sometimes not all people will easily read your limits and for this reason, it is important that you explicitly define the limits you can go and the limits that they are allowed to reach when dealing with you.

Even though it appears an easy undertaking, most individuals set limits but lack the spine to enforce such boundaries. Allowing other peoples to overstep and violate your limits will reverse all gains you have made in developing emotional intelligence. While pursuing the definition of limits allowable, it is important to be considerate and respectful of yourself and others. There is a difference between letting people know the limits allowable and imposing their limits on them. For this reason, effective communication is inherent in emotional intelligence. Remember negative emotions such as anger can be enhanced by failing to let others know of the allowable limits. Fortunately, like any other aspect of emotional intelligence, you can learn how to say no respectful and firmly.

"Anger is not a weakness, it is an emotion but the manner of handling it can be a weakness"

Earlier on, we extensively covered why it is important to acknowledge and express all emotions. If you accept that emotions are a form of energy then you will realize why it is important to express them because, in this way, you will dissipate the energy and attain equilibrium. We correctly argued that locking up emotions is counterproductive as at one point you will either experience an emotional outburst or you will act irrationally endangering yourself, others and the systems around you. Anger is a common negative emotion that many wrongly assume that it should be suppressed. In this book, we are arguing that anger should be expressed as an emotion but it should be expressed in when it is building up by various ways of managing anger such as breathing deep or counting up to one hundred before making a decision when angry.

"Sometimes spiritualism and culture can enhance or worsen emotional intelligence"

There are some religious practices that infuse aspects of meditation that can help an individual attain self-awareness. By understanding yourself, your strengths and weaknesses, you will begin the journey of improving your emotional intelligence levels. For instance, a saying a prayer may allow a person to engage in constructive soliloquy, which enables the individual to express his or her feelings instead of locking them up. On the other hand, some cultural practices may contribute to increasing emotional intelligence. For instance, Western cultures may encourage expressing of emotions while most African cultures demand that men bottle up emotions. However, it is important to remember that cultural influence is large to the environmental factors that may favor being expressive or reserved.

Expectedly, spiritualism and culture can also worsen emotional intelligence levels of a person. For instance, religious practice that qualifies negative feelings as expected norms that one should live with can aggravate poor emotional reaction to challenging situations. Individuals subscribing to such practices may not see the need to seek help as such emotions are qualified as expected and one should instead toughen up. There are cultures that frown at the thought of men exhibiting emotions especially negative emotions forcing such individuals to feel ashamed of being emotional beings. When you analyze the contribution of your spirituality and cultural influences to your emotional intelligence levels, you will pick what positively contributes to your emotional intelligence and drop others that aggravate inappropriate handling of feelings.

"Empathy does not imply forgetting self for the sake of others"

Even though we have emphasized the value of empathetic listening in developing emotional intelligence levels, it should not imply sacrificing your conversational needs for the sake of accommodating the other person. Empathy should involve active listening and trying to analyze the issue from your viewpoint and the viewpoint of the other person. For this reason, empathy does not imply letting go of your wealth of experience and opinions, it simply requires you to view the issues from two perspectives to enable you to make a fair conclusion. The other role of empathy listening is to make each participant in the conversation comfortable by eliminating a one-sided view of the situation.

"Avoid excuses as they equate to running away from reality"

At one point in life, each one of us may have resorted to excuses because they provided an effective way to avoid protracted conversation that might be difficult. Unfortunately, excuses are merely a cover of underlying issues and do not offer any real solution. It is important that you learn to face your emotions and their impact rather than justifying why you behaved in the manner that you did. Emotional intelligence offers a long-term approach to facing your fears and joys individually and in the public sphere. Excuses work against the spirit of emotional intelligence, as they are technically lies while emotional intelligence advocates for honesty and consideration of all parties involved in an interaction.

"Fortunately, emotional intelligence can be cast into a system approach to issues"

While human behavior is dynamic and unpredictable, emotional intelligence is highly predictable. Emotional intelligence can be seen as a universal template for expressing and managing each emotional reaction. This quality of emotional intelligence makes learning and applying emotional intelligence interesting as you can develop a custom approach to your emotions that is applicable to nearly all of your situations. As indicated, negative emotions and positive emotions are almost finite even though how we react varies. The variation to the way each person reacts to emotions varies but the common reactions are fairly predictable. All these attributes make emotional intelligence highly learnable and applicable by all persons.

"Like all learning and training, there are levels in emotional intelligence coaching"

When you start exploring emotional intelligence to improve your personality and character, remember that you do not have to learn everything in a day, month or year. Start by analyzing your strengths and shortcomings and focus first on your weaknesses. It is advisable to learn bit by bit according to your synthesis and application. With time, you can explore the entire spectrum of emotional intelligence including the areas that touch on your strengths. By accepting that there are several layers of emotional intelligence, you will focus on what you need and move on to the next when you have the confidence that you have gained much from the current level.

Chapter 5 Symptoms of addiction and tips for effective goal setting

Mornings might imply the bright beginning of a brand new day. However, for other people, when their alarm clock rings, it is a big confusion of moving yourself out of bed and going straight to the coffee shop. Though not everybody is a morning individual, beginning your day confidently is quite significant. Studies demonstrate that when you start your day in an encouraging mood, it boosts your probability of remaining cheerful as the day goes on. What you do in dawn might have an effect on the rest of your day. Therefore, why begin your day by waking up on the erroneous side of the bed? Generating excellent morning behavior does not automatically imply you have to wake up at 5 a.m. to set off to spin course group or do yoga schedule before job. There are small things you might do that take little time but might develop your mood, your routine, and your general happiness with your day. For those who are not morning individuals, there are habits to begin your day correct that does not even entail moving out of bed

Have you noted when your dawn begins by ignoring your alarm, missing breakfast, and hurrying out the gate, the rest of your day appears to replicate that mood of confusion as well? The nature of your morning shall decide the nature of your day. Consequently, it is time to begin scheduling accordingly.

When you structure well routine behaviors for the morning, you prepare your day for accomplishment. Whether you are conscious of them or not, you function under routine all the time. Part of increasing a strong routine is to be intentional with it. The majority of behaviors are formed because they are simple or along the lane of the slightest struggle. If you desire to develop positive behavior, then you might require putting several intentional efforts into structuring them until they become instant nature.

This is mainly right with morning behavior. What you nurture in the morning sway how you think, operate, and feel during the day. Below are easy practices that you might add into your morning habits, to guarantee you are feeling, behaving, and judging at your highest level for the rest of the day.

Avoid Technological Devices

If the initial thing people do when they wake up is checking their phone for e-mail or job message, they are doing themselves damage. They are instantly cultivating a reactive outlook, rather than a proactive one, which shall cause them to begin their day in a distrustful condition, rather than a position of internal calm and control.

As a substitute, try remaining disconnected from technology for the earliest hour of your day so you might start your day with present-moment consciousness and a constructive focus.

Take a Glass of Water

Taking a glass of water in the morning after going hours without taking is an excellent way to hydrate the body. The skill of adding lemon to a lukewarm glass of water assist eliminates toxins from the digestive system that might have built up during the night. Additionally, the technique provides a high-quality basis of vitamin C, assists in weight loss, and rouse metabolism.

Practice Cheerfulness and Gratefulness

Before you move out of bed, offer yourself a couple of minutes to smile and put into practice gratefulness. When you smile, it notifies your brain to discharge the feel-fine neurotransmitters. The released element boosts your humor, calm down your body, and lowers your heartbeat. Who could not desire to begin their day on this encouraging note?

As you smile, begin to reflect on the issues that you are thankful for before moving to the next subject. Studies have revealed practicing gratefulness lessens anxiety hormones and boosts mood. Consequently, adding a straightforward daily gratefulness practice is an enormous way to begin your day.

Start by taking a single minute in bed before you wake up to reflect on an individual and an occasion you are thankful for in your life.

Organize the Bed

It might appear like a waste of time, inconsequential, or pointless, but making the bed is an easy action you might take at dawn that makes you begin your day feeling accomplished. Moreover, that is a healthier tone to set that signifies a sense of self-importance and achievement. Taking control and completing easy tasks shall offer you the basis to take on more during the day.

Meditate

Including some sort of mindfulness practice such as meditation into your day-by-day morning schedule might assist ground you and prepare your mind and sentiments, which then sways how you respond to challenges during your day.

Throughout your meditation is a good time to state your purpose of the day. When you are clear on what you desire your day to progress or what you desire to feel or achieve, you might make clear decisions that generate the life you desire to live.

Below is an easy meditation you might do at dawn:

Put yourself into a relaxed seated pose and set a clock for ten minutes.

Close the eyes and concentrate on your breathing.

Breathe in through your nose for ten counts, maintain for ten counts, and breathe out through your nose for ten counts.

Each time you note your mind drifting, tenderly guide it back to concentrate on your breathing.

When the clock goes off, let go the counter, but remain seated with the eyes closed for a second.

Set a purpose for your day and picture yourself meeting this purpose.

Open the eyes, stretch your hands up, and then go on with the day, carrying the peaceful energy and meaning with you.

Exercise

Whether it is an easy yoga schedule or a fast stroll with your pet or a speedy set of sit-ups; starting the day with movement strengthens the body and the brain. Decide what type of exercise is correct for you and program it. It does not have to be complex, extensive, or extreme, but having some, type of physical movement in the morning shall make your blood moving and assist quiet any psychological chatter. You may switch up what type of exercise you do each day to keep your schedule appealing.

Compose Yourself

Putting your time and energy to your appearance assists make self-assurance. When you feel composed, it is one fewer thing to be anxious about during your day.

Consequently, bathe, clean your face, clean your teeth, make your hair, dress to strike, and use any other grooming routine that makes you feel excellent regarding yourself. This might entail picking out your attire prior to or ironing your outfit. Whatever makes an individual healthier, looking acceptable, and feeling positive plays a vital role during the day.

Eat a Well-Balanced Breakfast

You have noted that breakfast is the most significant dish of the day. When you take time to consume a strong breakfast, you shall have more liveliness during the day and a stronger aptitude to concentrate and focus.

Keep a Schedule

Take some minutes to note down a list of activities for the day ahead. Then categorize it so your day's directory has only three to five items on it. The list should be ranked in order of main concern to make sure you deal with the most urgent things first.

Scripting down your daily activities instead of having them floating in your brain assists clear psychological chatter. You as well offer yourself a sense of purpose every day when you distinguish what you require to be done. In addition, there is fulfillment regarding crossing off responsibilities on your list as it nurtures a sense of achievement.

Enough Sleep

Getting enough sleep is not a routine for your morning. However, before you may expect to put into practice new, strong morning practice, you must have the basis of a well-rested body and brain. The manner you feel whereas you are up is reliant on your sleep behavior. If you have been feeling tired, bad-tempered, or fatigued, you might not be getting adequate sleep.

Throughout sleep, the body is functioning to support a fit brain task and upholding your physical health. Sleep plays a fundamental role in your bodily well-being, psychological transparency, and superiority of life that ongoing sleep shortage might have unpleasant effects on your health. Additionally, good sleep enhances how well you feel, respond, work, study, and relate with others.

Bathe

Taking a shower has a method of shocking your coordination and getting your transmission going. If you completely cannot get yourself into the washroom, then at a minimum do a methodical washing of your face and end with a splash of freezing water. You will appear and feel more conscious than you could if you could simply walk out of bed.

Get up at the Correct Time.

We have all noted that morning individuals are the most industrious. According to several studies published by a number of emotional Associations, contributors who self-identified as morning citizens accounted for feeling better off and healthier. One theory from the study, however, is that the distinctive nine in the morning to five in the evening workday is geared to profit those who operate at their most excellent early in the day.

While it is right that several people who get up earlier are frequently more industrious, that does not imply night owls cannot have a fruitful morning that results in an industrious day. For night owls, mornings happen afterward, but maybe fruitful nonetheless.

People who work during the night shifts are productive and proud of it. Despite having, several sleepless nights, and poor sleeping habits, people who work during the night achieve their goals.

The most vital matter is not what time you get up, it is getting in harmony with your body's timer. Your body comprehends what it must be doing and when. Do not force yourself to be a member of the five am alliance if you cannot get sleep before midnight.

Getting adequate sleep and getting up when your body is prepared shall result in a more fruitful day than waking up hours before your mind is prepared. Walking up earlier than normal is a recipe for body burnout. In addition, the routine cannot go on for long. If you are not used to waking up early, you cannot force it and the body shall only operate with you for some period before it breaks down.

Reduce Decision-Making Responsibilities in the Morning

Occasionally the best technique to have an industrious morning is to get ahead begin on it the previous night. Several productivity specialists and flourishing individuals spend their evenings getting ready for the next day since it makes their mornings open to get a better start on a significant job.

Setting up the evening before is helpful because we have an inadequate amount of determination and decision-making capability every day. The idea of making several conclusions in the morning shall slow you down and exhaust your mind the entire day. If you may get rid of decision-making from your daybreak, you shall have more dynamism and time to have the most prolific morning you can.

Consequently, write down your daily schedule the previous night before. Pledge to the notion that the morning schedule might start in the evening. Select your attire set your lunch and your bag for the next day's work. If you fancy studying a book in the morning, choose it the previous night and put it somewhere noticeable so you spot it easily. If you desire to exercise in the morning, sleep in your gymnasium costume.

Do What You Adore

if your enthusiasm is playing football, writing poetry, or showing kids how to swim, take time to do it. You shall discover that when you are doing what you adore, you are occupied with happiness.

Assist Others

occasionally after we have accomplished our personal objectives, we still feel unaccomplished inside since we have not made a significant contribution to somebody else's life. When we help others, it sounds excellent to be of service to somebody else. The contribution we make seems fulfilling and is a huge potential basis for our cheerfulness.

Spend Your Time with Other People

When you share your feelings, your time, and your skills with others you feel good for it. Time spend without sharing may be lonely. When you spend time with other people, they will feel good towards you and assist you to have more happiness in your life.

Look for a Life Instructor

A life trainer shall assist you to assess your life and why you are not feeling joyful. Maybe have limiting thinking or you have a sentimental obstruct without understanding. By taking to a life teacher, you might discover why you are dejected and what you might do to feel good.

Give Handouts

You do not have to offer luxurious gifts; on occasion, a verse, a note, or a caring email shall brighten somebody's day. Share what you might offer to all the magnificent persons in your life.

Learn to Forgive.

Keeping a grudge shall hurt you more than the other individual. You should take notice of how you think when you release your rage. Concentrate on a good future and you shall feel good.

Take a Stroll in Nature

Walking in nature might be uplifting and renewing, particularly when you are living in an artificial world. Strolling in your neighborhood park and getting fresh air might let you understand the attractiveness of the natural world.

Generate a Daybreak Habit to Focus Your Brain

Perhaps the most significant constituent of an industrious morning is your schedule. Almost every productivity specialist suggests a morning schedule, though each one is just a bit diverse.

According to several productivity specialists and authors, the greatest thing you might do to be industrious is to make your perfect morning habit. Additionally, experts explain that how you begin your day anchors you and guarantees you concentrate on what is most significant. You have to master a dependable morning habit to attain your uppermost level of production.

Ideally, not every daybreak habit works for everyone; however, there are fundamentals that make the morning schedule most valuable. If you examine productivity specialists' morning schedule, you will discover a few components in common. They have a constituent of focus on large picture goals, gratefulness, and arranging for the days' time.

You might exploit output by investing the majority of your time and liveliness on those detailed responsibilities that shall generate the largest impact. Once you have completed those responsibilities, you might concentrate on other actions that are on your schedule.

Read Books

Reading books is a good technique for gaining knowledge and arouse inventiveness. Fascination reading develops concentration and has a soothing effect related to meditation. Additionally, reading prior to sleeping might assist you in sleeping well. True-life books are an outstanding instrument to widen the horizon, build up new ideas, and search for motivation. Additionally, they present actionable guidance on how to conquer all sorts of challenging circumstances through real-life instances.

Single-Tasking

Very few people on the planet might multitask effectively. While there is no damage in irregular multitasking, regular juggling between responsibilities limits your concentration and adds to psychological clutter by making it hard for your mind to filter out inappropriate information. Additionally, according to research, serious multitasking lowers competence and may damage your cognitive power. This is the reason you must single-task. Make a record of goals you require to achieve in a day. Begin with what is most significant and scroll down the list, finishing a single duty at a time.

Appreciate

It is easy to be trapped up in the rat contest and overlook how lucky you are. Practicing appreciation is a good technique to generate positivity, lessen stress, and boost your physical wellbeing. How can you nurture this healthy routine? Institute a gratitude diary, volunteer, take time to value your treasured ones and tell yourself of at least a single subject you are thankful for each day before going to sleep. The more you value the small happiness of life, the better you will feel.

Associate with Constructive People.

You are the average of the ten individuals you share the majority of your time with. This is accurately why you must cautiously think about whom you are sharing time with. Avoid affairs that let you down rather than uplifting you. In addition, share time with individuals who understand how to cultivate and share cheerfulness. Because cheerfulness is infectious, it is one of the easiest means to generate constructiveness in your life.

Listen

Successful communication is decisive when it comes to nurturing individual and professional affairs. In addition, listening is fundamental to communication. It shall not only make other people feel cherished but shall also assist you to comprehend them better and attain a fresh outlook. Do not try to control the discussion or false attention while your brain is busy guessing what meal you must order for dinner. Pay attention to what they have to state and what they signify and notice the non-verbal prompts as well. The better you pay attention the more you shall learn..

Avoid Social Media

The social media world has taken control of almost every part of our daily lives. The average individual has seven social media platforms and utilizes at least an hour and thirty minutes each day on inspection social media platforms. Studies indicate that the more hours you waste on social media platforms, the more prone you are to grow depression. Consequently, it is advisable to cut out the use of social media to lessen anxiety and psychological disorder. Put off your telephone and computer for several hours each day to develop your frame of mind and reconnect with the people around you.

Self-Care

Taking time off to relax might be good for your frame of mind, psychological physical condition, and sense of worth. Practice at least a single thing each day that makes you feel excellent. Listen to good songs, study the latest skill, take a long shower, or make a pleasant meal

Chapter 6 Reduce Stress in the Workplace

- There is no "right" or "wrong" way to practice meditation as long as you are getting results. However, there are so many different types of meditation technique (some of them also have different sub-branches) that you may find yourself overwhelmed when trying to decide on the best one for you.

Again, don't get lost in the details. Yes, many techniques appear to be intricate and confusing when you start getting into the details but actually, they are very simple when practiced gradually. It is sufficient to know the basic types of meditation in order to decide on the best method for you. You also need to have a basic knowledge of how different techniques affect the brain in different ways. Moreover, don't let the exotic names overwhelm you either. The meditation techniques presented here are much easier than their names imply! To follow is a brief summary of 12 different meditation practices and their benefits.

Body Scan Meditation (Progressive Relaxation)

The goal of this meditation is to mentally scan your body for areas that are tense (Where the flow of energy is blocked) and to release or relax the tension.

The meditator usually begins the body scan from the feet, moving slowly up to the head, or vice-versa.

Some methods involve tensing and releasing muscles during the san, or visualizing a gentle wave or waterfall washing over you and clearing the tension.

It helps to alleviate pain and promote relaxation, calmness and sleep.

Mindfulness Meditation

The goal is to help the mind become aware and focused only on the present moment.

It diverts the brain's focus on negative thoughts, modifies rash reactions and impulses, improves focus and memory and keeps you on the present rather than dwelling on the past or fretting about the future.

Most other meditation methods incorporate some mindfulness techniques

Breath Awareness Meditation

This a great meditation for beginners. It is a mindful technique that promotes mindful breathing.

The goal is to focus on the breathing while releasing any other thoughts that come to the mind.

It reduces anxiety and improves concentration and mindfulness.

Kundalini Meditation

It is known alternatively as Kundalini Yoga and said to be the most powerful of Yoga methods which achieves the fastest results.

Practitioners are encouraged to visualize Kundalini as a coiled serpent at the base of the spine. The serpent symbolizes the latent power we all have inside of us and the goal is to "awaken" the serpent and access its power.

The goal of this method is to channel your energy in order to relieve stress. We have 7 energy centers throughout our bodies called chakras. It is believed that energy from the root chakras at the base of the spine must be channeled through the other chakras and released through the crown chakra at the top of the head to revitalize the mind and body.

This is a physical type of meditation that combines deep breathing with yoga movements and the recitation of mantras.

This type of meditation typically requires a teacher who leads the students in the various movements, although it is possible for an experienced meditator to it on their own.

It improves physical strength and flexibility, can relieve some types of pain and reduces anxiety and depression.

It strengthens the nervous system and boosts creativity

It teaches proper breathing techniques and enhances ling capacity

A 2008 study found that the regular practice of Kundalini meditation alleviated chronic back pain and increased the energy levels of participants.

Ideal for people who want to combine exercises with mental relaxation.

- 5. Zen Meditation (or Zazen)

It is the main method practiced by Buddhists and is derived from the ancient Buddhist tradition dating back to the 7th century.

It involves numerous steps and specific postures, therefore, it is best practiced under a master

It is very similar to mindfulness meditation. The goal is to concentrate on the breathing, and on releasing ant thoughts that come to mind without judgment.

It helps increase awareness of how the mind works.

It relies primarily on the movement of the breath with the belly.

There are three main methods of Zen meditation; "observation of the breath", "quiet awareness" and intensive group meditation.

The advanced form of Zen meditation requires a good master and a committed student.

Practitioners of Zen meditation have reported improvements in blood pressure, anxiety levels and depression.

Transcendental Meditation

It relies on slow, deep breathing whereby the person is able to rise above or "transcend" his present state of being.

A mantra is used during the meditation in advanced techniques under a master, this mantra is determined according to specific factors, such as birth dates. On simpler methods, the person may choose the mantra of is preference, such as, "I am empowered" or "I am one with the universe".

Practitioners of transcendental meditation may have deeply spiritual experiences that transform their lives.

- Qigong (Chi Gong)

This is a method that originates from ancient Chinese medicine and is translated as "life energy cultivation.

The goal is to unify the breath, body and mind in order to achieve a perfect balance of energy or "Chi".

This is another method that relies on physical movement and is practiced by coordinating slow specific movements with the breath to achieve awareness and calm.

In the west, Qigong is practiced more as a relaxing exercise rather than a meditation.

It contains stages where one starts with the basics and gradually moves to more advanced stages and therefore, it is best to learn under a teacher or instructional CDs.

- Taoist Meditations

An ancient Chinese meditation where the goal is to attain harmony with "Tao" or nature.

It combines visualization, mindfulness and contemplation techniques to achieve this harmony.

Taoist meditation contains a variety of branches, the most commonly known in the west is Qigong. Other branches include "Internal alchemy",, "Guide and pull" and "Great ultimate fist".

- Vipassana Meditation

    - IT is the oldest of the Buddhist practices and is said to be a method developed by the Buddha himself.

    - The goal of this meditation, also known as "insight meditation" is to attain full awareness of events as they are happening.

    - Behind this method lies a deep philosophy, where awareness is used to gradually break down the wall of illusion that separates one from reality – and from our true selves. It is a long process but in the end, enlightenment and liberation are attained.

- It is arguably one of the hardest methods. It follows a very specific system of steps and exercises to train the mind and takes years of cultivation of a very high degree of mindfulness.

- Ho'oponopono Meditation

This is not a conventional meditation but a Hawaiian ritual that has its roots in the accident Polynesian tradition. The term in Hawaiian means

"to put to rights" or "to correct", or "to tidy up".

It was traditionally a family ritual of healing and forgiveness and therefore cannot be practiced by a person on his own. Traditionally, extended family members would meet daily or weekly to perform this ritual to settle existing problems and prevent future family troubles from occurring. Other families would meet only when someone became ill. The believed that illness was caused by breaking the spiritual laws through anger, guilt or doing harm to others. A priest would be called to lead the ritual of forgiveness and making amends, or an elder of the family would lead the meditation.

The goal of Ho'oponopono is to mend broken family relationships and maintain harmony among all family members.

The ritual starts with a prayer, followed by a statement of the problem. Family members then discuss the problem and how it should be corrected. The discussion is interspersed with periods of silences during which each person reflects on the wrongdoing and their emotions. Forgiveness is then acknowledged and everyone "releases each other", letting go of any anger and hurt and the matter is closed. The ritual is then followed by a meal which typically includes seaweed, a symbol of the release.

This is one of the least practiced methods although the philosophy behind it is very beautiful and profound. Some native practitioners provide this meditation to clients as a form of family counseling.

Dynamic Meditation

This a contemporary method developed by western practitioners to address our sedentary lifestyle lack of physical activity. It is very suitable for people who want to de-stress in a more active way.

It starts with body movement and progresses to the calming of the mind.

It is said to be a breakthrough in modern meditation methods as it relies on vigorous movements rather than focus and contemplation to achieve the same results as 'sitting down' meditation.

Meditation Yoga

Yoga is a form of meditation and is one of the oldest traditional Hindu practices. It was introduced to the west by Indian yoga gurus who came to visit or migrated to the United States and Europe.

There is a wide range of Yoga practices and methods, but the one most commonly practiced in the west relies on a series of postures called "asanas".

Today, Yoga has become more of a physical fitness and body strengthening technique that relieves stress more than a self-awareness and contemplation method. But in many traditional schools it still revolves around spiritual goals.

Loving-kindness Meditation

The goal is to increase empathy and compassion towards others and is very beneficial for anger management.

It helps develop more positive thoughts through self-acceptance and compassion towards oneself, which in turn will extend to others.

It is practiced by focusing on thoughts of kindness and love, first towards oneself and then gradually, extending those feelings to include others. These 'others' progressively include a friend, an acquaintance whom you feel neutral towards, then someone whom you dislike and so on, until your loving kindness is able to encompass all beings and the entire universe.

The method may sometimes be accompanied by a mantra or visualizing the suffering of others and wishing them well.

Christian Meditation

The goal of this method is a deeper understanding of God, and the purification of the soul to attain closeness to God.

Some methods of Christian meditation are called "Christ Consciousness" and their goal is to raise awareness of Christ and His presence in our lives.

"Being with God" meditation involves focusing with the entire heart, mind and soul on God and feeling His presence around us.

Another method, contemplative prayer, involves the repetition of a devotional prayer.

Sufi Meditation

Sufism is a mystical tradition within Islam Its practitioners were regarded as heretics because they sought to attain mystical communion with Allah through the purification of the soul.

Many Sufi practices were influenced by Indian Yoga.

The main practices include reciting mantras, contemplation of God, heartbeat meditation (focusing on the heartbeat rather than the breath) and a whirling ritual where meditators whirl to loud drumbeats and religious music to achieve a form of "Nirvana"

Which type of meditation is best for you?

The above types of meditation are by no means the only ones. Many of them have different branches, while others can either be practiced very basically individually or more intensively with a teacher. Some teachers also combine techniques from different methods to form their own "brand" of meditation. How should you decide which method will work best for you?

If a certain type resonates with you. This is a very valid reason. If it appeals to you, you are more likely to stick to it and practice until it becomes a habit. The philosophy behind the method may appeal to you, you may prefer more mindfulness-based methods or a more physical type that incorporates some kind of yoga.

What specific benefits are you looking to gain? Do you need to improve concentration, sleep better, have more energy or control a craving? Having a specific need or goal is a good way to narrow down the choices.

How often can you practice? Ideally, you should meditate every day and if you do have time for that, you may find that the short, mindfulness-based breathing meditations work best for you. If your schedule simply does not allow for daily meditations, plan for twice-weekly or thrice-weekly meditation sessions and in this case, you may choose a longer and more intense method.

Well, actually, it is all in the head when you think about it, but the results are concrete. Scientific data has shown us the has dramatic impact of regular meditation on mental and physical wellbeing almost from the moment you start practicing; and that the longer you continue to practice, the more time you put in, the more benefits you will see.

If you pursue meditation with the sincere intention of attaining clarity, self-awareness and mindfulness, you are already halfway there.

Chapter 7 How to declutter your mind and positive effects

Overthinking results in Procrastination!!!

Are you thinking so much about your future? Perhaps you need a new career, become healthy and sick-free, or begin investing for the coming years or even build your own company.

The reality is that, when the time comes, somehow you get stuck in your head, in your thoughts and find it hard to handle your thinking.

You tell yourself, I just do it the next day, and then the next day never comes. Prior to knowing it, you are stuck in that hideous cycle PROCRASTINATION without end approaching.

Anticipation Can Kill You!!

Are you familiar with Garfield, thinking about the mission of getting out of exercising? According to Garfield, "Perhaps I must get up and work out, but my feet will begin to hurt, and my heart will beat faster. I will get out of the air, begin to sweat, and I can't make it back home. Work out is not so bad, he added, But anticipation is killing me!"

Like him, the things you have to perform perhaps are not so bad; however, your anticipation is killing you. The small initial step could have a remarkable effect on your whole life, so you over-analyze it. Overthinking results in Procrastination, destroying your inspiration to take a step towards doing the things that you like to be doing.

Over-Analyzing Things Is Unhelpful and Destructive

I experience this last year when is started my own business. The first thing I did was to set up a Facebook page; it was not easy for me as I was over-analyzing the situation. There are things that keep on lingering in my mind like, will people appreciate me or reject me? Am I fit enough? What if I can't make it? These questions and overthinking lead me to procrastinate. It takes me weeks to set this up. So, you see, overthinking is destructive. It doesn't provide any benefits and doesn't help us to move forward. Overthinking can also result in other unenthusiastic and unhelpful feelings like anxiety and stress. I was strained and worried during these six weeks.

- WHY Overthinking?

Why we over-analyze things? What are the best ways to stop Procrastination from taking place?

There are lots of reasons WHY we overthink everything, and one of these is a lack of self-confidence. Once we hesitate and are irresolute, we let uncertainty and fear to creep in our minds. Perhaps FEAR is one of the important reasons why we overthink.

We have lots of fear such as fear to lose, fear of change, fear of failure, fear to be discriminated, fear not to be accepted, etc.

Worrying is also an important reason why people overthink. Even if worrying is a natural response to new and unidentified things, in our culture, we often think about how can things go the way we expected. Then, this can attract issues in it.

Overthinking is also considered as a security, secure us from nuisances and dangers.

Another important reason why we overthink is that we are continuously searching for and striving for flawlessness. A perfectionist is always planning to do something better and bigger. This can result in a high level of stress and anxiety as she or he overthinking the way to be great and wonderful. This way of life can harm your mental and physical wellbeing and health. Keep in mind that nobody is perfect and you'll never be. Therefore, when you accepted this, then you maybe end your pattern of thoughts. After all, thinking a lot is a bad habit that can stop us from having a happy and fulfilling life.

- How to Deal with Procrastination

If you are familiar with the pressure, constant worry, and pain which goes along with leaving things to the last minute. Although you want to complete or accomplish a task, you tend to have an issue on how to get it started. There are lots of ways which can help you deal with Procrastination. This can help you avoid possible Procrastination in the future.

- Technique #1: Changing Your Point of View

Stop Exhausting Yourself for Procrastinating: If you are exhausted, you will find that it is so hard for you to complete the task. Don't blame yourself if you made some mistakes. You need to move forward and concentrate on the things you have right now.

Disappointment and guilt can drain your energy and emotion. Wasting time howling at yourself for not completing your manuscript will make frustrated and extra tired. Also, it will stress you out, tend to make it unfeasible for you to complete your homework at that time.

Do an Essential Task for Fifteen Minutes: Rather than wasting time thinking on the total number of hours you are about to work for, why not start it immediately. Tell yourself you have just fifteen minutes to complete it. This will cope with the fear factor and tend to spend a lot of time on your task before stop working again. Just in case fifteen minutes sounds too intimidating, do something for only five minutes.

Break Your Tasks to the Easiest Down to the Hardest

It is overwhelming to think about completing an entire manuscript or getting in a whole week's worth of task. Rather than overthinking everything you need to carry out like one significant hindrance, why not break them according to complexity and deadline. You can start from the easiest down to the most complicated one.

Like for instance, rather than thinking, I have to complete this task before midnight, why not tell yourself, I am going to finish this task slowly but surely.

Think about trying a specific method like Pomodoro, wherein breaks occur at predetermined intervals.

You have to keep away from creating a disorganized, and extended to-do list. This is only setting up yourself for failure. Rather, make subcategories such as Fun, Home, Loved Ones, and Career and try to cross off some entries from every list daily.

Begin the Day Tackling the Most Complex Jobs

Create a schedule in the morning and choose the most complicated task first. You will be more energetic in the morning, most especially if you have a sound sleep and eat your breakfast. Engage yourself in the most laborious task, and you will feel good and blessed one it is completed. Afterward, start doing some of the simplest tasks.

Know when you are most alert and motivated and plan out your day; as a result, you utilize this time best. Like for instance, if you are a morning individual, do the most difficult task after you wake up. But, if you are likely sleepy and slow in the morning, there is a chance of making careless mistakes or irritations by going headlong into a tricky task.

Self Talking for Some Motivation:

Self-talking is an excellent way to make yourself calm down, focused, and reached your objectives. Tell yourself you can do it. If others can, you can do it as well.

Self-talking by saying like, Pearl, I know that this past few day has been hired for you and you are exhausted. You have written lots of articles in the past, and you are going to write more.

Also, you can ask yourself a question like, Pearl, why you are feeling nervous? You have the talents and skills to handle it.

Talk to yourself louder. It will work in your head if you are in an open place.

Make Sure You Completed the Project Even If It Is Not Perfect: Imagining the perfect assignment, essay, article, or project could be what is stopping you. It is nothing at all if it not completed. Therefore, abandon your fears (or vision) of the best products. Also, you aren't able to fix what does not present yet.

Promise yourself you will get a prize when it is completed: Perhaps you are dreading the next, but a lot of hours you have to complete the project. Tell yourself that when it is done, you get to rejoice with one of your preferred things. Make use of your expectation to push yourself in pain.

- Technique #2 Eliminating Distractions from the Surroundings

Choose a Perfect Workstation

Know where you will be carrying out most of your job, and make it the best excellent setting for the limited interruption. It's especially significant to have a devoted workplace that is diverse from the one where you unwind and calm down.

This place might be a coffee shop, library, local bookstore, or home office.

Install an Application to Keep Away Phone InterruptioN

Usually, smartphones are the black holes which drain off our attention and time. Yes, there is a specific app for that. Download and install an app that will solve your procrastination issue the best.

For instant fixes, consider the AppDetox.

Yelling Mom enables you to set a time for the application to begin nagging you to start something.

Procraster app prompts you to recognize the primary source of the Procrastination and then provides you recommendation concerning the issue problem.

An easy timer app can be utilized to assign how long you planned to work then how long will be your break. Once the timer is up, switch tasks rapidly and sticks to the plan.

Use a Browser Add-On or Program to Keep Away from Internet Interruption

If your problem is constant browsing, download an app to solve your addiction to the internet. There is an array of programs available for Mac and Windows OS. If you have self-control, then set a time prior to go on time-wasting sites and go back to work when the time is up.

You can try Freedom for all operating systems and devices

Self Control enables you to obstruct a list of sites

Eliminate your mobile phone from the place if you want to: In case you are not able to control it in a similar position as something which is going to entice you, solve that issue by keeping it in another space or switching it off. Also, this goes for another device like iPads and computers.

If you want to keep your mobile phone on for work or family-related reasons, switch off all the notification apart for calls and texts.

Listen to Instrumental Music

A lot of people find it hard to work and keep focused on a silent space. However, if you're listening to the melody that has lyrics, you will almost surely get preoccupied with the words. Opt for instrumental music or a white-noise machine.

- Technique #3: Keeping Away from Procrastination Long Term

Set a Goal by Creating a Record of Things that Need to Be Done

Make a list of the projects you have to complete. The list must take account of short term project you have to complete every day and every week and long term projects that might take a couple of months to complete. Seeing those goals in a paper will help a lot in planning the different actions required to reach your objectives.

Although you make use of your gadget for your other records, from birthday wishes to groceries, avoid putting this list on there. Jotting down your projects is key to thinking on how to accomplish them.

Prioritize Goals with Deadlines

To quickly and effectively schedule your time, it is advisable to make use of a planner. Put down short term projects in daily or weekly lists which take account of a cut-off date for every item. Set cut-off-date for long term projects by recording them in monthly entries.

Include the whole thing you wish to get accomplished in your daily planner

Like for instance, on Saturday, your science project is due. Reserve at least two nights to complete the project. Also, you have got to go to the department store to purchase a vitamin before leaving for a vacation. This can be done on Wednesday night.

Try utilizing an Eisenhower Box technique for effectively prioritizing tasks. Usually, you classify or sort out the things you need to be done into four categories, such as:

- ☐ Projects that should be completed right away

- ☐ Projects which can be completed later or re-schedules

- ☐ Projects which can be assigned to somebody else

- ☐ Projects which are not essential and can be removed.

The strong point of this technique is that it functions well with the projects you should be done in a given day, but also on a longer timescale, such as weeks and months.

Keep Away from Multitasking to Concentrate on One Project at a Time

Multitasking makes one feel like accomplishing a lot. However, it stops you from completing tasks effectively and quickly. Keep your focus on one project at a time as this will help in avoiding you from getting overwhelmed by a hectic schedule.

Get a Company or A Buddy

It is hard to keep away from interruptions and do the job on time when you are doing it by yourself. Unluckily, we fight with Procrastination. Ask members of the family or a friend if they would be willing to work with you to check in on each other's job habit and achievements.

You can schedule a fun outing with your buddy for meeting your goals. Once you keep procrastinating, stop the outing as a penalty

Chapter 8 What is Mindfulness

Coming to terms with procrastination and overthinking starts with finding out where they come from. As with any psychological issue or concern, the answers regarding origins and what lifestyle points might affect them will be different for each individual. Fortunately, modern psychologists and health professionals have spent plenty of time studying these behavioral phenomena and the amount of knowledge related to overcoming them has grown exponentially in the last few decades.

Through various studies and surveys, professionals across the globe are discovering and sharing their findings with regards to who is most at risk for developing psychological habits, how to identify them and how they can be treated. As with any medical or health-related topics, not all symptoms and traits are going to be true for every person who struggles overthinking or procrastination habits. The point of gaining this knowledge is to determine which factors or variables each individual is facing so that a plan can be formed for how best to tackle their personal situation.

Now that we've provided a better understanding of what overthinking and procrastination are, let's take a closer look at where they come from and what types of personalities are more likely to cave to their emotionally driven psychological compulsions.

What Causes Procrastination?

If procrastination is something that everyone has to deal with at multiple points throughout their life, can it really be all that bad? Despite the many health and well-being risks associated with habitual procrastinating and overthinking, there are still those who refuse to believe that their personal habits and compulsions are under control and far from being dangerous to their mind or body.

Pro Tip: This denial is one of the challenges all people wanting to take control of their habits and behaviors must overcome before any forward progress can be made. If someone is unwilling to acknowledge their issue and make a conscious decision to change, then they are not going to be able to improve their behaviors or psychological habits.

However, there is plenty of hope and proven techniques out there that have made all the difference for those wanting to give up procrastinating and overthinking. The most recent studies have shown that the development of habitual procrastination can be traced back to four main psychological causes:

Unable to Focus or Gain Control of Thoughts: Sometimes people who have difficulty with controlling their thoughts or getting themselves to focus have their behaviors being controlled by their emotions rather than their logical thoughts. Emotions are truthful and powerful, but they are also unpredictable and capable of changing without warning, especially for those with existing psychological conditions.

Fear of Failure & Fear of the Unknown: These are perfectly natural phobias that every person faces at some point in their life. While for many the fear disappears once a plan has been made or more information has been gathered, but for others these types of fears (which can be encountered in nearly any given situation) can lead to full-blown panic attacks and other emotional reactions can affect their behavior and inspire psychological habits like procrastination and overthinking to take control of all thought and action.

Lack of Motivation & Low Levels of Energy: These two traits are often connected as many who find themselves trying to cope with procrastination also have experience with larger psychological concerns like depressive states, suicidal behaviors in extreme cases, and the development of anti-social behaviors related to lack of confidence or faith in their own talents, abilities or future potential. This negative thinking constantly circling through their mind can leave damage on an individual's self-esteem, a negative emotion that comes with physical side effects such as fatigue, low immune system efficiency and muscle soreness throughout the body with little to no physical strain to cause it.

Need to Reach Perfection: This is a common trait that comes with the fear of failure and is one of the main causes of procrastination. Through their previous experiences with procrastination and their tendency to overthink, they begin to believe that the only way they will be able to complete something or come to a proper resolution is if their application is totally flawless. Of course, perfection is an often impossible bar for people to reach, particularly when distractions, interruptions and unwelcome challenges can arise at any time and throw off even the most well-planned solutions.

There are still those out there that argue habits like procrastination and overthink cannot be nearly as harmful as people claim they are since everyone deals with them at some point but not everyone falls prey to their control of behaviors and reactions to situations throughout life. Recent studies have looked into this fact as well as determined that the reason not everyone develops dangerous psychological habits because there are those in the population that are more susceptible to the negative and long-term effects than others.

In the following comical chart, it is easy to see the type of distracting thoughts and actions people take when avoiding their tasks and responsibilities, along with the fluctuations in stress levels that come with giving in to habitual procrastination.

While the image itself may have a comical tone, it is an accurate and widely relatable visual of the types of thoughts that dominate someone's mind when procrastination habits have control over a person's mind, emotions and behaviors.

What Kinds of People Are Most Likely to Become Procrastinators?

Like with all psychological habits and behaviors there are some with different personalities and lifestyle variables that can be more or less likely to develop procrastination or overthinking habits. Some of these common variables and personality types include:

Perfectionists: People who struggle with being a perfectionist often also have difficulties controlling their impulse to procrastinate. One of the main reasons for this is because people who take pride in perfection and faultless execution in everything they do are less concerned with not getting a task done than they are finishing something that is flawed in any form. However, for many procrastinating perfectionists, the closer their deadline comes or the higher the pressure gets for them to take action, the more panic sets in an they find themselves in a panicked frenzy to complete their task.

Students: Students, regardless of age or education level, are some of the most common victims of procrastination and overthinking. One of the reasons for this is often connected to a lack of confidence in their own talents and abilities that causes them to obsess about each and every detail of their assignments until they are trapped in a whirlwind of thoughts that keeps them from completing their task. Another one of the main reasons for student procrastination is the self-deception that comes with the belief that they perform better under the pressure of a nearly impossible deadline. Despite being told over and over by their friends and family that they will not only feel better, but that the quality of their work will improve if they didn't procrastinate, the impulse is too strong in many cases and the need to put off their responsibilities takes over.

Pro Tip: Those who use this excuse are able to convince themselves that they will be able to complete their task to their best ability even in the shortened amount of time typically because they have done it before. It only takes one successful event for the habit to start and take control. The first time someone procrastinates and is still able to complete their task or find their solution in time for someone to start procrastinating as a matter of habit and compulsion.

People Pleasers: Those who find themselves constantly surrounded or often outnumbered by people who are difficult to please often become procrastinators. These types of people are eager for those around them (both peers and superiors) to see them in a certain light. It could be that they lied or fictionalized something about themselves in order to paint this picture for their friends or co-workers, or it could be that there is no reason for the person to feel inferior to those around them because they are just as experienced or talented, but do not see it because their self-esteem has been so wrecked by their procrastinating and overthinking habits.

Those Who Have Learned Through Experience: Those who procrastinated until they were under the gun and managed to come out on top without consequence once or twice by accident are more likely to develop a problem with habitual procrastination because their experience has taught them that they are still able to put out quality work or make solid decisions without having to spend the effort and energy on the time management skills and patience it would take to achieve their goal in a timely and comparatively stress-free manner. While they may consider themselves lucky at first, the longer this habit is allowed to develop and is practiced by the individual, the further the quality of their work and performance (often in various aspects of their life) will slip until those they work or interact with take notice and action.

The Connection Between Procrastination & Overthinking

While the two are often symptoms of a larger psychological concern that should be acknowledged and explored, habitual procrastinating and overthinking have also been linking as being the cause for one another. Overthinkers who consider themselves driven and motivated in everything they do find that over time, their psychological habit of obsessing over small interactions or replaying regrets through their mind can develop into habitual procrastination over time as these individuals try to find ways to distract themselves from their dominating thoughts and emotions, often pushing aside responsibilities or pressing tasks to avoid having to think about them.

Alternately, those who start as procrastinators may find over time that they are overthinking more and more about the things happening around them, personally and professionally. One of the main reasons for this is that those who are self-aware enough to recognize their impulse to procrastinate in matters from choosing where they want to eat dinner to delivering a major presentation to their employers are also emotionally intelligent enough to realize that the anxiety and panicked emotions that come with that habit are only increasing their stress and decreasing their chances of success. Unfortunately, although they are aware of their habitual procrastinating and overthinking, the compulsive behaviors associated with those habits are more powerful than rational thinking and are often determined by how the individual is feeling at any given moment. This only makes the habitual overthinking worse as it brings up questions like why the person can't just make themselves take an action or make a decision and why they start procrastinating every time they face something, knowing how much stress, regret and guilt comes with the process.

Another connection that is common between the development of procrastination and overthinking habits is a third psychological stage that is fueled by emotions like the fear of failing and the awareness of passing time and burning energy that could be used more productively. This stage is an overwhelming guilt that also comes with negative health and wellness effects like fluctuating stress levels and uncertainty of one's ability to accomplish anything.

Use This Newly Gained Knowledge & Get the Answers You Have Been Searching For!

Now that the knowledge has been collected, it is time to put it to use and start preparing for those first steps forward with taking control of your mind, behaviors and emotions in order to conquer your habitual overthinking and/or procrastination.

As with any plan, the first step is to take a step back and analyze the situation as a whole. Answer these questions about yourself or the person you are concerned for to get a better read on the big picture and the individual factors that may affect treatment:

What behaviors have you noticed that could be connected to habitual procrastination or overthinking?

What is the individual's personality type? Do they fall into the category of higher risk personalities?

What specific factors could be causing the habitual procrastination or overthinking?

Are there certain situations where their behaviors, thoughts and actions (or lack thereof) can be identified as compulsive or driven by emotion rather than rational decisions?

Have you (or the individual in question) acknowledged and accepted that there is a problem with these habitual compulsions that is hindering their ability to function at their full potential?

The Origins Have Been Explored. Traits Have Been Analyzed. What's Next for Breaking These Habits?

Now that the foundation has been laid for better understanding of psychological concerns like procrastination and overthinking habits and information has been shared about who is statistically most likely to develop these habits over others, it is time to start making an actionable plan for how to change the way the mind thinks and views the world so that impulses like procrastination and overthinking lose their power over your behaviors. Answer the following questions to determine whether or not you are prepared to begin taking control of your mental and psychological health in order to improve the health of your whole being:

Have you fully acknowledged your individual negative psychological habit or multiple habits?

Are you prepared to make conscious decisions and alterations to your behaviors and reactions?

Can you stick to these changes, overcoming your emotional impulses that may arise and challenge your determination?

Are you ready for a better life packed with as much fulfillment, success and discovery as you can fit into each day?

If the answers to these questions are all yes, then it is time to get started and time to take control of any and all psychological behaviors to make the most of life and everything it has to offer!

Chapter 9 A simple guide and techniques on meditation and its benefits

The decisions you make today do not only affect the present, they also set the tone for the future. Make better decisions today!

How often do you make decisions? Every day. No matter what we answer, though, that's the reality! We are always compelled to make decisions, though the nature of our decisions differs greatly. For example, there are big decisions and small decisions. Small decisions shouldn't take much time; big ones may take days or even weeks. And yet, we can't avoid it; we must make those decisions. However, before any decision is made, one must consider some essential factors.

Indecisiveness is a negative trait that could slow down the entire decision-making process. Most people aren't proud of the fact that they are indecisive. An indecisive person might pressure others to decide for them, either indirectly or directly.

For these people, making choices themselves can be a scary thing since they will keep asking themselves: What would eventually happen if I make a bad decision? It's normal to be fearful when you are making the decision yourself, but know that as you continue to do this, you will trust yourself more, and you will practice the act of making big decisions.

And the more you keep making significant decisions yourself, the more you will be glad to exclude other people from the decision-making process; you will need their approval less.

Therefore, since the basic idea is to make decisions yourself, independent of anyone, the following tips will help you to make decisions easily and more quickly. Consider the following six methods:

Be Aware of What You Want

One of the ways to identify what you want is to determine what your goals are. When you become more aware of what you want in life, and when you decide what your goals will be, it is evident that you will be able to make better choices. David Welch, a political science professor whose work was published in the Huffington Post, says that people who aren't self-reflective will undeniably end up making bad decisions because they aren't aware of what they want in life in the first place.

Therefore, when making a decision, you should ask yourself where you want to be next year and if that decision will help to take you where you want to go. If your answers are quite different from what you are working towards, then the best thing to do is to make a different decision. So, the critical point here is to identify what you want in life.

Ask for Advice, but Make Your Own Choices

Admittedly, making a decision doesn't mean that you should not seek advice from others; after all, no one is an island of knowledge. But you should be cautious; this could be a decision regarding your relationship, your well-being, or your job. Do you feel comfortable confiding in others and asking for their advice?

Others may not understand exactly how you feel, but should that be a reason why you shouldn't seek advice? No! You can gather information from them and make your final decision yourself. It is also important to remember that you are ultimately the one who will have to live with your decision.

Pay Attention to Your Gut

Yes, we all know ourselves better than we realize. But in some cases, most people ignore the message that their gut is telling them since they don't want to hear the consequences their decision will bring or deal with the reality of it. It is essential to be objective and clear-headed each time we are faced with some difficult choices, such as making big decisions.

Therefore, when you are making a tough decision, it's ideal to write down everything you are thinking and the reason you think you are feeling that way. As you begin to have an internal dialogue with yourself, you may become lost in an endless maze of thoughts. By writing down your thoughts, you will strengthen your conviction and are more likely to listen to your gut.

Ensure That You Are in the Right State of Mind

A person who isn't in a good mood will find it tougher to make the right decision. Unpleasant feelings that could influence the decision-making process include stress, hunger, and drowsiness.

Take, for instance, if you are trying to figure out what you will eat for lunch when you are hungry, how easily will you be able to decide? And this is a relatively small decision.

Therefore, to avoid being rash, when making a big decision, you should ensure that you are feeling comfortable and emotionally balanced. Then, after these criteria have been met, make your decision.

Learn to Trust Yourself

Don't confuse trusting yourself with arrogance and having a big ego. Experts have said that the first person an individual has to trust is himself/herself. Just because you believe in yourself doesn't make you arrogant and proud.

No one could be as consistently supportive of you in the same way that you will learn to be. Then how do you accomplish trusting yourself? Be kind to yourself; when you do, it boosts your self-confidence, and you will not need to seek approval from other people before you make any decision.

Trusting yourself, too, will let you make a sound decision eventually, even after meeting people for advice. Also, when you love and care for yourself, your connection with others becomes strengthened. Don't forget that it's a task to have the strength to trust yourself. So, as soon as confidence is met, then you will be pushed and thus be courageous to make big decisions in the future.

Practice, Practice, Practice

The way you get improve is by making your own decisions every day. If it becomes part of your day-to-day routine, you will have more confidence in decision-making and taking inspired action will get easier and faster.

According to psychologists, mastering the process of making the right decisions is depends on a lot of factors. They include a person's developmental age or stage, their idea of what's right and wrong, and their understanding of what the decision-making process entails.

Since you are unfamiliar with making big decisions for yourself, try it for a week, and don't ask anyone else to make your decisions for you. As you gradually improve, then it will become part of you, and thus you will be in control, without the influence of another person.

With these six tips, what's the bottom line? To be good at making big decisions, you really must devote a lot of time and practice. And the moment you are there, you are your own boss.

How to Stop Expecting the Worst

Have you ever thought about what keeps our brain from behaving logically? It's fear! Why? It's because fear looks so real and essential that if we dare ignore it, something terrible might happen. And that's exactly the scenario that occurs when you are expecting the worst. You are trying all you can, but it's just resulting in a magnification of your fear, anxiety, and stress.

Here is an anecdote that will explain this phenomenon further. One man said: Generally, he usually looks at his rearview mirror many times before he gets home. He knows that it's not the best thing to do, but he said he thinks doing that is the best way to be conscious and know if someone is tailgating him, and he mentions that it annoys him to see people following him.

So, one night, as he was driving home, he notices that a car is following him closely; the vehicle keeps in close contact with him, following in him every direction he goes. And after making a few turns, he started to get suspicious and asked himself: Is this person following him? Was he seen entering his car? Could they be a serial killer? Is he their next victim? Many questions were flowing, but he couldn't answer them. Maybe he's watched too many true crime shows?

He convinced himself to think positively and think of ways that he could resolve his situation. He could drive past his house so that he could fool them to disallow them from knowing where he resides. To him, it seemed like a good plan. Then something happened next.

After his next turn, he noticed that they went in a different direction; he kept going, and nothing showed up. At that time, he realized that they weren't following him anymore. What did he do next? He breathed a sigh of relief, and now he felt that it was ridiculous for him to think that they were following him.

In the real sense, that is what happens when you are anticipating or expecting the worst. At that stage, your body starts to panic; you breathe faster, your heartbeat quickens, and you start to breathe more shallowly. You will start to picture horrific scenarios in your head and alter your behavior as a result of that fear.

What happens to you during this period will affect your mood and stress level, and negatively impact your ability to make good decisions. So, how do you stop expecting the worst? Let's expand on these four points sequentially.

1.Identify Your Fears

First, you have to ask yourself: When you are always expecting the worst? Are those times when you deliver a presentation at work, when you are writing an exam, when you are keenly worried about your loved one's safety or your own, or when you are participating in social interactions? Yes, there are many things that could make you be fearful; identify them.

When you determine some specific scenarios, then you will have a higher tendency to identify where your fears lie and what your beliefs are about certain situations. The more you can be aware of what triggers your anxiety, thus making you expect the worst, the more that you will have the strength and power to stop it. So, don't hesitate to take a moment to reflect on when you are usually expecting the worst and why you are doing so.

If you have generalized anxiety, it's likely you expect the worst-case scenario. In that case, you are always anxious, overwhelmed, and stressed, and your heightened arousal will affect your thinking; you are more likely to overestimate adverse outcomes. Here are a few questions to ponder:

Reflection Questions:

- When do I expect the worst?

- How do these affect my emotions, thoughts, behaviors?

2.Challenge Your Expectations

Of course, when you expect the worst, your mind will always tend to create unreasonable and unrealistic scenarios. Honestly, we're blessed with the ability to imagine; it inspires wonder and creativity. The downside is that when we expect the worst, we don't always consider the facts of the situation and relative probabilities of all possible outcomes.

So, when imagining an adverse event, our fear could become so all-consuming that we will neglect the facts and fail to look at the reality. This is normal, though. But we mustn't forget that this comes from our basic need and desire for survival. To preserve our own safety, we are inclined to overestimate the tendency that bad things will happen.

Take, for example, many people who are afraid of flying. When I flew on an airplane recently, we had some turbulence, and a woman who was sitting next to me was nervous and held onto the chair that was in front of her due to fear. Like her, many other people were worried. And it's understandable; whatever happens in an airplane is definitely not in your locus of control.

However, the odds of dying in a plane crash are 1 in 11 million. You are far more likely to be either hit by lighting or be severely attacked by a shark than you will die in a plane crash. How does that make you feel? So, these facts could correctly be used to challenge the logic behind your fear.

3.Get Your Feelings Out

Emotions and thoughts can be so toxic if you have no outlet. Therefore, it is very advisable to journal and use other artistic methods to process your emotions in the right way, and that will help you to feel better.

So, write down your thoughts in a journal so you can speed up your recovery. Don't keep anything inside just because you would feel embarrassed if someone else were to read it. Also, you may speak with a trusted confidant if you would feel more comfortable doing so.

4.Take Control

To take control, you need to begin with what you have control over. As difficult as it may be to do so, it is important to let the rest go. When you sit and ponder the worst-case scenario, you are not helping yourself. So pay attention only to things you can do.

There are lots of things that you can't control; a list will assist you in clarifying them in more detail. Here are two important ones:

- What other people feel, do, or think about you.

- Situations that you have no control over.

Thus, when you focus on what you can do, you will boost your confidence level, and there will also be a decrease in your stress level; you will be able to take confident action when and where it is necessary, without overthinking.

The following four points highlight some of the best reasons why you should be able to stop expecting the worst-case scenario.

Worrying Does Not Solve Problems

Worrying does not provide you with any benefits, nor does it solve any of your problems. Don't fool yourself by thinking that the more you worry about a situation, the more you will work toward achieving it.

When you do, you are only making yourself unnecessarily stressed, tense, and anxious, which negatively will impact your ability to think critically. Therefore, each time you think about the worst-case scenario, ask yourself: Is this really helping me? It does not, and this is the first important step to mastering your thoughts, reducing your overthinking and anxiety, and improving your life.

Chapter 10 How to Stop Overthinking

A cluttered mind has no space for anything new. Often, when you feel that your mind is in a state of overdrive, it prevents you from enjoying the opportunities that life has to offer. Overthinking will put you in a constant loop since you feel like you can't stop yourself from ruminating over a certain issue. The worst thing about this is that there is minimal action you can take to solve the challenge that you are experiencing. As a result, overthinking only damages you as it holds you back from living your life to the fullest. This chapter looks at practical tips that you can incorporate into your life to help you stop overthinking.

Learn to be Aware

Just like any other problem that you might be going through, the best way of solving it is by understanding the causes of the problem in the first place. With regard to overthinking, the first step towards dealing with it is by recognizing that you are overthinking. It is important that you live consciously by knowing what is happening in your mind. Any time you feel overwhelmed and stressed, you should take a moment to analyze the situation that you are going through. Your awareness should denote to you that these thoughts roaming in your mind are not helpful. Enhancing your level of self-awareness will help you stop yourself from thinking too much.

The following pointers should help you to boost your self-awareness.

Meditate

Today, millions of people value the importance of meditation. Usually, meditation stresses on the aspect of focusing on a certain mantra or your breathing. Meditating regularly increases your self-awareness since you connect with your inner-self in ways that you haven't done before. Meditation will help you connect with your inner self. Accordingly, practicing self-talk keeps you motivated on the goals that you have set for yourself.

Know Your Strengths and Weaknesses

Another effective way of increasing your self-awareness is by knowing your strengths and coping with your weaknesses. Undeniably, as humans we are not perfect. The strengths and weaknesses that we have affect how we work towards our goals. In this regard, most people will only focus on doing the things that they are good at while doing their best to ignore their weaknesses. Knowing yourself better ensures that you don't waste your time and energy doing activities that will only make you feel negatively about yourself.

Know Your Emotional Triggers

In addition, it is essential that you know the emotional triggers that frequently influence your reactions. By knowing these triggers, you can catch yourself before overreacting. Moreover, your self-awareness can be helpful here as it guarantees that your emotions do not overwhelm you. Instead of reacting without thinking twice, you can stop to mull over a particular scenario and act accordingly.

Practice Self-Discipline

Every day, your life will revolve around things that you wish to accomplish. Achieving set goals can be a very positive experience. However, this doesn't come easily. You have to be willing to pay the price. This means that you should learn how to effectively control yourself and focus on what's more important. This is what self-discipline is all about. You should be ready to do anything that brings you closer to your goals.

Try New Experiences

There is a lot that you can gain from life when you learn to value the importance of new experiences. Think about it this way - the more you know, the more you find different ways of approaching life and solving the problems you are facing. Don't limit yourself by going through life with the same perceptions and doing the same things over and over again. Frankly, this will make every aspect of your life boring. So, go out and have fun. Try new things and challenges.

Motivate Yourself

We all need motivation at some point in life. When you are motivated to do something, your mind has the energy it needs to see through a particular challenge. Therefore, motivation warrants that you embrace positivity in spite of the problems that you might be going through. Indeed, this also has an impact on your self-awareness since you are surer about yourself and your abilities.

Get a Second Opinion

Earlier on, we had pointed out the fact that overthinking can be caused by overcommitting yourself. Maybe this is something that you are accustomed to. We all know how it feels when you manage to successfully complete a project on your own. However, at times it is important to recognize that you can't do everything alone. As you might have heard, "two heads are better than one." Save yourself from the nightmare of weighing your options on something over and over again. Just ask someone else for a second opinion. You will be surprised that you can easily solve a problem that once appeared too difficult for you. Therapy works in the same manner since you get an opportunity to talk over your thoughts with an expert.

Stay Positive

When you are constantly worried that something could go wrong, your mind will race through varying thoughts trying to figure out the best possible solution to solve your situation. Instead of paying too much attention to the negative, change your thoughts and reflect on all the good things that can happen to you. Savor these moments and help your mind adjust to the fact that you can also be happy. Develop a habit of encouraging your thoughts to stay positive.

Identify Distractions

There is a common phrase that goes "what you resist persists." In line with the habit of overthinking, trying to prevent yourself from thinking about something only makes you think too much about it. As a result, the best way of stopping this is by doing something more engaging. Go for a walk with friends. Learn to play a new musical instrument. The point here is that you should make an effort to distract your mind.

Stop Being a Perfectionist

Evidently, there is a good feeling that comes with knowing that you have done something perfectly. Nevertheless, it is quite demanding to do things perfectly all the time. In your everyday life, you should leave room for mistakes. This ascertains that you will not be frustrated when something goes wrong. Focus on learning from your mistakes. Ultimately, you will notice that you start paying less attention to doing things perfectly. This creates room for more opportunities since you will be willing to try anything, whether you succeed or not.

Set Deadlines

Spending too much time thinking about a decision can lead to overthinking. Some decisions do not require you to think too much about them. They are simple choices that you can make within a short period. Therefore, it makes sense to set deadlines that you will make a specific decision before the end of the day. Depending on the importance of the decision, you should set ample time to ensure you end up making sound decisions.

Surround Yourself with the Right People

At times, it is difficult to think positively if the people you surround yourself with frequently have negative thoughts. If you spend most of your time with people who are always worrying, then you can be sure that you will also find yourself worrying. On the contrary, if you surround yourself with people who always think positively, you will also be influenced to have this perception about your dreams and aspirations. Therefore, you can help stop overthinking by choosing to spend time with productive and positive people. They will help free your mind from worrying about what the future holds for you. With their positive energy, you will appreciate the importance of living in the present.

Do Your Best

When facing new challenges in life, it is a common thing to see most people worry about what they can and cannot do. Unfortunately, this worrying attitude prevents people from handling challenging situations effectively. When faced with difficult situations, it is imperative to focus on giving it your best without thinking too much as to whether you got it right or not.

You never know, there are certain situations when the outcome is not as important as you thought.

Create a To-Do List

We can attest to the fact that there are instances when the mind tends to blow things out of proportion. Have you ever heard your inner voice try and convince you that you cannot complete a certain project within a specified period of time? Frankly, this happens many times where the mind jumps to the conclusion that you have more things to do than you actually do. The funny thing is that the mind will even go to the extent of giving you reasons why you cannot complete the project. To prevent this from happening, you should learn how to work using a to-do list. A to-do list keeps things organized. It guarantees that you can handle one task at a time without making it seem too burdensome for your mind to tackle.

Cut Yourself Some Slack

The desire to succeed might be too ingrained in you that you cannot think of anything else that is not related to what you want. This leads to a scenario where you are too hard on yourself. You will find it difficult to forgive yourself for the little mistakes that you make along the way. Unfortunately, this leads to overthinking.

The truth is that you can't always expect that things will go your way. We are human beings and therefore, we are prone to making mistakes. Successful people understand the importance of making mistakes. It gives them an opportunity to identify their weaknesses and work on them before reaching their goals. Imagine if people only succeeded without making mistakes. Mistakes should be perceived as a stepping stone towards success. As such, always remember that being too hard on yourself is damaging.

On a final note on how to stop overthinking, you should bear in mind that anyone can be a victim of overthinking. We all yearn for the best in life. Therefore, it is okay to overthink things from time to time. However, this becomes a problem when it develops into a habit and you feel as though you cannot do anything about it. Your self-awareness, for example, will come handy each time you slip into a state of overthinking. Additionally, looking for positive distractions can encourage your mind to think about other things instead of sinking into your thoughts. More importantly, you should always remember to seek a second opinion from those around you. There is a good reason why we have friends and social circles. They should be there to help you offload thoughts and emotions that seem to weigh you down. Talk to your loved ones and if there is no one to talk to, you can always engage in self-talk.

Conclusion

But you now know-how.

Having read this book besides having learned that overthinking is habitual.

You have begun to now understand that overthinking can come from a wide variety of areas in our life. Most importantly how things like having a boor sleep habits can affect and even make existing overthinking worse.

By understanding this problem at the basic level, you are much more likely to avoid encountering the many different issues that are associated with overthinking. See because overthinking functions as a habit it can seem at first very challenging to break that said habit.

But now you should understand how to break bad habits.

By eliminating things that cause a negative influence on your life you can further yourself. We all know that there are many things in our lives that can have a negative influence on us. But trying to break this influence is often a challenging ordeal, many times we find that in trying to break a bad habit we can sometimes end up developing a worse habit as a result.

This is where understanding the basics of habitual behavior comes from if you do not understand how a habit is formed and how it can play into overthinking you are going to be doomed to continue the process of overthinking. Knowing how a negative influence can cause you to overthink and how as a result your thoughts can begin to become cluttered allows you to take the high road out. When viewing overthinking just as anxiety what can begin to happen is that you will get this black and white view of it.

This misses the many nuances that are associated with it, something as complex as our mind is not going to work in such a simple paradigm it is going to be influenced by many different factors, and this is the case for something like overthinking.

Finally, with learning how meditation works you now have the best defense against overthinking that you can ask for, a time-tested method that has been used by people all around the globe for generations to combat their anxieties and worries. That is what meditation is in the most simple and short definition it is not some kind of esoteric practice, it is a simple calming method. With all of these tools now at your disposal, you are better prepared than ever to combat against overthinking.